PRAISE FOR

It's *Never* Personal

"*It's Never Personal* is humbling, has a lot of heart, is deeply relatable, and is a true original just like its author. The book offers truth-seeking readers a unique and original combination of spirituality, ancient wisdom, psychology & neuroscience. This book compassionately gets to the root of why we take things personally. By putting into practice the Never Personal Process, the reader is encouraged to become more curious versus reactive and just may be forever changed in the way they view forgiveness, the self and the other. This is a book to revisit and savor time and time again."

—BECCA TAFT, LMHC,
BECCATAFTCOUNSELINGSERVICES.COM

"This book is a gift—a practical guide to a deep sense of freedom. Vicki leads us to a truer perspective that honors the personal experience while releasing the grip of unnecessary suffering. It's not about indifference, but about becoming empowered. If you've ever struggled with taking things personally, this book is for you!"

—KATIE DEASCANIS, LMHC

"*It's Never Personal* by Vicki Kennedy would be a good read for anyone considering enhancing their progress in therapy and getting back control over their lives. She is an excellent therapist and educator. I deeply admire her dedication to excellence, her wisdom, and her ability to explain complex things in a simpler way.

This book could be a great asset to anyone working on how to stop taking things personally and take back control of their lives. Vicki does an excellent job explaining the mechanisms of how these beliefs and behaviors originate and how to get out of the trauma vicious cycle. Her book explains and breaks down blocks on the way to freedom from the past burdens. Great read; would definitely recommend!"

—ALY LANDRY, LMFT, LMHC, NCC

"In her book, *It's Never Personal*, Vicki has tackled an issue that hounds us all. Cutoff and disconnection in key relationships is as costly as it is common. It's the deepest pain humans can feel. And most of the ways we cope come from good intentions, but produce bad results. We blow up or shut up; we go ballistic or go away. And along with that comes the self-doubt and self-talk... that we're too much... or not enough, that somehow it's our fault or we caused or deserved it. Deep down, we all are our own biggest critic. We indeed take it personally... and end up stuck. Letting go of all that is truly our life work. Vicki makes that work easier through her own insights and experiences... vulnerably, sincerely, and honestly.

Through sources of wisdom, both ancient and modern, from science to philosophy to theology, Vicki helps us heal, forgive, and just plain travel lighter through life. She shows us that, indeed, what we hold onto holds onto us: shame, resentment, defensiveness, and negativity; she helps us find our truer, more authentic self.

Vicki has been a professional colleague and personal friend for ten years now. We've co-facilitated couples workshops together, and I've seen her passion for her work, her growth, and for those she serves. This book brings that value to a much larger audience. Thank you, Vicki, for sharing a part of your journey with us and for helping us to learn the power of letting go."

—MARK W. BECK, M.DIV., M.ED., LMHC, LPC

"*It's Never Personal* doesn't just offer psychological insights—it offers a path to enlightenment. With rare clarity and compassion, Vicki bridges the realms of psychology and spirituality, delivering a roadmap for releasing deeply ingrained patterns that keep us stuck in cycles of suffering. She writes with such profound wisdom that once I started reading, I literally could not put this book down.

This book is an essential read for healers, spiritual seekers, and anyone who has felt the rejection and heartache from taking things personally. Vicki shares a powerful 5-Step Process that helps untangle the inner workings of why we take things personally and gently shows us how to shift into a place of real freedom; as she beautifully puts it, 'there is nothing to forgive.'

In a time when many of us feel powerless or triggered by others, *It's Never Personal* is a much-needed reminder that the path to peace starts from within. Vicki's voice is truly a gift."

**—LESLIE LARSON, MS, PSYCHOTHERAPIST,
CERTIFIED HYPNOTHERAPIST, AND
CERTIFIED GESTALT THERAPIST**

"Vicky has ambitiously taken on such lofty subjects as religion, ancient wisdom, Epigenetics, psychology, and more, deftly weaving them together with vulnerable, personal stories that will help readers understand and relate. Her audience can trust her not only as a well-read researcher and therapist but as a real human being who has worked hard to overcome her suffering. For a therapist to reveal they are also human (we all are, by the way!). This in itself is highly therapeutic. Vicky generously normalizes our shared human experience of pain and rejection and also points toward the path to healing.

This insight-laden book offers more than theory but also step-by-step strategies and concrete 'Points of Contemplation.' The author artfully blends an array of some of the most widely regarded therapeutic modalities with ancient wisdom traditions and offers her own 5-step process.

The scope is breath-taking and effective. Thank you, Vicky, for adding to the field with this expansive, heartfelt guidebook for healing our interconnected heart, mind, and body."

—JILL HAMILTON BUSS, LICENSED MENTAL HEALTH COUNSELOR

"*It's Never Personal* is more than just another book—it's a profound invitation to return to Self. With extraordinary depth, clinical insight, and soulful compassion, Vicki guides us to unravel the protective narratives we've built and meet our emotional pain not with fear, but with compassion, courage, and clarity. This isn't a book that simply informs—it transforms.

Through vulnerable stories, reflective insights, and practical tools, *It's Never Personal* offers a deeply nurturing roadmap for healing. Vicki masterfully blends clinical expertise with heartfelt wisdom, inviting us into a journey of true integration—from rawness to awareness, from fragmentation to wholeness.

As a fellow therapist and privileged to know Vicki as a trusted colleague and a cherished friend, I can say wholeheartedly that she lives what she teaches. Her grounded presence, unwavering integrity, and deep discernment make her one of the first people I turn to when my emotions are hijacked, and reactivity takes the lead. Reading this book feels like sitting across from Vicki—grounded, perspective, and authentically attuned with a rare blend of insight and uncanny humor.

It's an honor to endorse this transformative work—and the luminous soul behind it, my dear 'Bella Chica.'"

—TEONA KIM ALEXANDER, MA, LMHC, NCC

"This book is an essential reading for counseling practitioners, clergy, and educators, but equally valuable for anyone seeking to heal wounds we carry and have struggled to release. Particularly, her 'widening the view' approach transforms our capacity for empathy, even toward those who have hurt us or differ from us. In a world that often feels divisive and frightening, she provides a roadmap for recognizing our shared humanity and how our nervous system responds to connection, showing how relationship repair guides us back to wholeness."

**—DR. GEORGINA PANTING, PROFESSOR
OF COUNSELING AND MENTAL HEALTH,
COFOUNDER OF EIRENE COUNSELING SERVICES**

"In *It's Never Personal*, Vicki plunges you, the reader, into the depths of your longing to be "free from suffering" and "fully alive" as a human being made in the image of God and designed to "love well"—beginning with God, then yourself and others!

The five-step process (NPP) she details in this book describes the essence of "letting go" and living in the reality of "true forgiveness" (not spiritual by-passing) and experiencing a life lived from true identity rather than the false self. I especially appreciate the vulnerable sharing from her own life—Thank you Vicki!!"

**—ROGER SHEPHERD MA. MA. LMHC,
PRESIDENT OF FLORIDA COUNSELING**

"As I moved through the pages of *It's Never Personal*, I was captivated by Kennedy's multifaceted approach to conceptualizing and healing from the psychological and relational wounds we all experience. She provides a practical model designed to enhance one's internal and interpersonal functioning.

Furthermore, this dynamic narration elicited a deeper sense of Spiritual and Existential reflection, wherein I utilized the steps in this model, considering the needs of my deeper self. This book personally spoke to me about my wounds, my relationships, and my existence."

**—DR. JEREMIAH STOKES, LMHC,
PSYCHOTHERAPIST, PROFESSOR**

"*It's Never Personal* is a soul-stirring guide to healing the emotional wounds we carry from betrayals, rejections, and the pain we've taken to heart. With clarity and compassion, the author offers a transformative roadmap for anyone stuck in the cycle of hurt, resentment, or shame. The 5-Step Nothing Personal Process is a masterful blend of psychological insight and spiritual wisdom—practical, relatable, and deeply empowering. This book isn't about quick fixes or empty advice. It's about finally understanding why we hurt—and how to release the burden in a way that honors our story and restores our peace. If you're ready to stop carrying pain that was never yours to hold, this book is the companion and guide you've been waiting for."

—DR. MARNI FEUERMAN, LICENSED PSYCHOTHERAPIST AND SELF-HELP AUTHOR

"This is an excellent resource that was written in a practical and accessible language while offering deep insights. A must read!"

—DR. JAVIER SIERRA, LMHC, LMFT, EIRENE COUNSELING SERVICES, INC.

It's
Never
Personal

It's *Never* Personal

Weaving Psychology, Neuroscience, and Ancient Wisdom Through a 5-Step Process to Finally Let "It" Go

M. Victoria Kennedy, LMHC

It's *Never* Personal:
Weaving Psychology, Neuroscience, and Ancient Spiritual
Wisdom Through a 5-Step Process to Finally Let "It" Go

For permission requests, contact: TheBirdsEyeView8@gmail.com

www.VictoriaKennedyAuthor.com

First Edition

ISBN: 979-8-9987052-0-5 (Paperback)
ISBN: 979-8-9987052-1-2 (Hardcover)
ISBN: 979-8-9987052-2-9 (eBook)

Library of Congress Control Number: 2025909422

Editor: Cindy Childress, PhD
www.cindychildress.com

Cover Design and Interior Formatting: Becky's Graphic Design,® LLC
www.BeckysGraphicDesign.com

Printed in the United States of America

This book is for anyone who has ever felt powerless over gripping emotions stemming from negative beliefs of self. May you be encouraged in these pages by the roadmap to complete peace and freedom.

Contents

Foreword

When I picked up *It's Never Personal,* there was an immediate resonance within me, bringing tears to my eyes. I have witnessed Vicki Kennedy in her client work and in our EMDR community, and her compassion, dedication, commitment to excellence, and authenticity consistently shine. Her tireless search for healing tools—for herself and her clients—comes from an indomitable belief that we enter the world whole and that no matter how we've been bruised or shattered, we can restore that sense of wholeness. She extends this hope to all of us through the lens of not taking things others say or do to mean anything personal.

As the owner and clinical director of Kimball Counseling Associates in Winter Park, FL, I regularly witness pain and despair inflicted by others within abuse survivors, those reeling from toxic relationships, and individuals with all levels of trauma. For them, as for many of us, wounds from the past are starkly visible, with the old negative self-beliefs and feelings of powerlessness and shame smashing into their present lives. Then, the cut of a careless remark, sting of a criticism, or a disdainful glance in our direction may never seem to clear. If it does, we wonder when that blow will strike us again, becoming preoccupied, blaming or hate ourselves, and believing our visceral responses as gospel. Yet, we yearn to move forward from the negative beliefs instilled in us as a very young, helpless, and vulnerable child. . . but how?

Through her Never Personal Process (NPP), Vicki maps out a blueprint for letting go of making sense of the past so we can be free of it, transforming our relationships and our lives. She illuminates this path by uniquely highlighting attachment theory, neuroscience, *and* spiritual teachings, demonstrating a constellation of causes and effects that shape our identities—and which we can manipulate. Far from being victims of our circumstances, Vicki reveals how our early interaction with caregivers impacts our brain development and significantly affects how we relate to others in adulthood, empowering us to rewire our brains and strengthen our human and spiritual connections. We methodically engage with parts of self injured in childhood through the steps of her NPP, bringing about healing and building our free will to create healthy relationships, which we all crave.

She paints a compelling picture of how we might let go of things we've taken personally through her personal stories and those of her clients. I immediately recognized my experiences in those stories, sometimes bringing me to tears, and other times, chuckling. Turning the pages of this book, I appreciated the power of Vicki's easily applied teachings and the Points of Contemplation that close each chapter; these provide guidance to work through each chapter incrementally on your timetable, by yourself, or with the help of a skilled trauma therapist. The book is well-suited to solo reading and study groups. I imagined my clients reading this book together, dropping walls of self-defense and encouraging each other, shouting, "Me, too!" and "That's me."

This book can enhance and even speed up the therapy process, giving readers the courage to look at their past with fresh eyes, then casting that view toward their future where they no longer take things personally. Are you ready to experience this freedom? Join Vicki as she guides you on this next phase of your healing as you discover that *It's Never Personal.*

—Diane Kimball, LMHC, *Certified EMDRIA Therapist and Approved Consultant, Kimball Counseling Associates | Winter Park, FL*

The Journey Starts Here

"In a dark time, the eye begins to see."

—THEODORE ROETHKE

It's Never Personal invites Wisdom Seekers and spiritually minded people to be curious about the betrayals, heartbreaks, and offenses that never seem to heal—not fully—because they felt "personal." As a psychotherapist in private practice, I've seen first-hand how clients are gripped by the pain, frustration, and confusion surrounding the topic of taking things personally and not knowing how to reconcile the grievances. Stories of suffering that span decades are so common. Individuals endure years of a narrative rattling around in their brains like a broken record without understanding how to reach true peace. The words from parents years ago that still sting, the friend who betrayed us, the boss who chose a colleague for the promotion instead of us, the ex who chose another over you. The lingering upset is deeply painful, heart-wrenching, and distressing. I feel the heaviness with them as they attempt to find a way to forgive.

You may have picked up this book to repair an intimate relationship where trust was broken or you feel betrayed. For others, you want to address a slow burn of offenses piling up when that person you care about lets you down—*yet again*. Or maybe a co-worker or someone in your friend circle always seems to rub you the wrong way. Some of you want to change how your mood is hijacked by strangers who cut line at the grocery checkout or disagree with you on social media. These are all things we take personally, and many of us struggle not to hold a grudge, no matter how empathetic and compassionate we usually are. We're burdened with insecurities of thinking "it must be me" when we feel hurt by the actions of others. This leaves us wondering: *What are we bumping up against in the heart, mind, or body that keeps us feeling grievously wronged no matter how sincerely we want to forgive?* We need answers.

As you might imagine, this type of deep work usually chooses us, rather than us spontaneously coming to the desire on our own. Not many people would be just lounging around the house looking for a project and say, "Huh, instead of cleaning out that cluttered kitchen drawer, maybe I'll plunge into the psyche today and see what I find to improve my experience in this life!" More likely, life pulls the rug out from underneath us, and we're flung into this work, or we have a lifelong theme of strained relationships and are grasping for an emotional handle we can grab on to and find relief. There's a hurt we've taken so personally; it opens a chasm between the self and the other that feels impossible to bridge. Yet bridging it feels as necessary as breathing.

Taking things personally and feeling unable to forgive can hold people captive in guilt, confusion, and shame that we're still upset and can't just "let it go." Faith leaders will tell us forgiveness is a virtue and quote the Bible: "It is right and good to forgive your enemies." The admonition is right and true, yet wholly insufficient and incomplete. If forgiveness were that easy, therapists' schedules wouldn't be stacked with clients caught in a quagmire of wanting to forgive the perpetrators but still feeling under attack emotionally long after the events in question.

Well-intentioned friends advise us to "let it go," "get over it," "be the bigger person," or say, "there are more important things in life to be upset about." Were those words comforting? Did they feel superficial and short-lived? You deserve meaningful, lasting calm and peace, and you know that doesn't come from cliches and maxims. You may have tried yoga, meditation, and talk therapy but remained frustrated. Listening to personal development podcasts and reading self-help books might help you feel better for a while, but the high soon wears off like cheap perfume. Perhaps you found Attachment Theory interesting but were left with more questions, feeling that there's something inside that you need to fix.

You don't need more advice on the importance of letting things go or recitals on the benefits of forgiveness. The answer isn't a mental illness label or picking apart the dysfunction in a relationship. How can anyone hope to experience lasting peace after being profoundly hurt if we don't know what that process looks and feels like? We're clearly missing steps on the path to forgiveness, and they're found in understanding why we take some things so personally to begin with.

WHY READ THIS BOOK

This book responds to the question, *What keeps us stuck in things we take personally, and how do we find freedom from the shackles of our hurt feelings to live fuller lives?* After listening to tens of hundreds of stories, I've observed that nothing cripples the human spirit as much as holding onto things we take personally. This is due, in part, to the secondary effects of holding onto grievances. You'll learn about those effects, including how:

- Our creativity is squelched, and our energy is misdirected when we allow words and actions from others to shape how we view and feel about ourselves.

- Unreconciled grievances morph us into stunted versions of ourselves, setting us up to never realize our full potential and forge paths we were never meant to take.

- Taking things personally darkens the heart and distorts our view of ourselves and others, impacting every area of our lives.

- We turn a critical, contemptuous eye towards others or take on a self-critical inward view in the form of shame or self-contempt.

- Our inability to release and process grievances shackles us to a life less than God intended, dreamed for by us, or imagined by our younger selves.

The losses are great, resulting in anguish, torment, and even depression. However, with the framework I outline in this book, you can avoid those pitfalls and navigate emotional disturbances when you're on the receiving end of an offense.

After all, the human heart wasn't designed to withstand the burden of hurtful feelings from rejection or abandonment on this side of Eden. And yet, these feelings create much of the misery and suffering we encounter in this life. You'll learn why we turn an eye inward to connect with the source/root of our pain and the origin of where, why, and how taking things personally began. Through this inquiry, you'll find the steps to free yourself from the paralyzing feelings of separation and shame from taking things personally. But not in the traditional way, which often bypasses the much-needed steps on the journey to a place of true understanding. You'll grow in knowledge of forgiveness from every angle, arriving to a place where you can truly embody the words, "there is nothing to forgive."

This book charts a psychological and spiritual perspective of your painful stories through the five-step Nothing Personal Process (NPP), inviting you to free yourself from feeling like a victim and move on. You'll learn about each of these steps in detail:

1. Identify Raw Spots

2. Hold and Release

3. Integrating the Whole

4. Widening the Lens

5. Birdseye View

Those steps create the pathway of identifying the source of our insecurities, integrating parts of ourselves that hold onto pain, letting go of distorted views of self and others, and finally experiencing true freedom through forgiveness and letting go of things you've taken personally. For those who choose this journey, there's potential for achieving your best self, or self-actualization, where you may find inner peace because you no longer blame yourself or the other—because you know "it" was never about you.

While this pathway to forgiveness stands on solid ground with the fields of neuroscience and psychology, I've woven in philosophy and ancient wisdom, including the Tao de Ching, the Bible, and Buddhism. I draw richly from *A Course in Miracles* by psychologist Helen Schuman, which I first studied in my 20s, informing my perspective on the spiritual dimensions of opening our hearts and seeing what really matters in the greater scheme of the universe.

You'll also find relatable examples, practical lessons, and meaningful tools to transcend what we may consider to be "unforgivable." At the end of each chapter, there are Points of Contemplation questions for you to journal and notice how the teachings may apply to your concerns. Along the way, I share the wisdom and experiences I have gathered, not only as a professional psychotherapist, having helped hundreds of people navigate this issue, but also as a fellow human working through the most intimate and painful things I've taken personally.

It is worth noting that some children experience events that could be classified as atrocities (such as sexual and physical abuse). Those acts hold an element of evil that doesn't just bend and distort our views of self and others; it crushes the spirit to a degree that feels almost irreparable. While this book doesn't directly tackle the intricacies of healing from this depth of human betrayal and trauma head-on (different degrees of trauma carry varying degrees of pain), it does provide wisdom and tools for healing the pain that burdens all humans around betrayal at all levels.

This book chiefly concerns itself with the merit domain of offenses that bring about suffering for humanity in general, with dings of unworthiness and doubts about our value along a continuum unique to each person's experience. Regardless of a pain's origins, the human spirit always seeks higher ground in the way of healing and redemption of the self. The Never Personal Process offers powerful and necessary steps to reclaim shattered pieces of the self in a way that honors the tapestry of our lives, redeeming our stories and those of others.

MY STORY

My motivation to write this book stems from my personal story of pain, disillusionment, disappointment, and heartbreak. I, like you, have walked through the fire. I have slogged my way along the broken road of rejection and abandonment. I have endured the darkness and confusion, tasting the sting of rejection and abandonment more times than I could count. I'm no stranger to the utter pain that comes from the blows of being left by a spouse, rejected by a friend, treated unkindly by colleagues, and feeling alone on the life's dance floor of emotional longings and needs being unmet, both by parents and other attachment figures.

I know well how solutions and resolutions that seem so complete in a therapy session can wear thin when we're out in the real world—even for me, a therapist. I've investigated the crevices of my psyche through intense therapy off and on for decades to heal the wounds of childhood that have unrelentingly clung to me. After all this time and all this work, there are still encounters when I struggle to figure out the riddles in relationships. Fortunately, with the tools in this book, I've found a pathway to cut through the pain and heal the cavernous pit of insecurity I have carried for most of my life.

You'll discover how I navigated events I took personally to let those hurts go, ultimately, and attain freedom. At least, mostly. I haven't yet arrived. Neither will you, because the forgiveness journey never ends. And yet, I've done enough work that when I get the ding or sting, I don't sit with it; instead, I quickly soar to the birdseye view that there's nothing to forgive *because whatever happened isn't—and never was or will be—personal.*

Perhaps this book may save you years of suffering unnecessarily. You, too, may apply and taste what it feels like to be completely present in the experience of "there's nothing to forgive."

CHAPTER 1

A Disturbance in the Force

"Things don't happen in a vacuum."

Both personally and through the clients I serve, I've had countless opportunities to investigate our "offenses" or "personal attacks," plunging into the underpinnings of this painful theme. Suffering has a way of forcing us to search for answers. I have explored taking things personally from every angle to make sense of the suffering and why we struggle to forgive those types of events.

This chapter explores what happens when we take something personally and the origins of this instinct, rooted in neuroscience and Attachment Theory. With this new understanding, you'll peel back layers of unintended consequences when we can't let things go.

WHAT HAPPENS WHEN WE TAKE SOMETHING PERSONALLY

We take things personally when we're dumped or fired, and our life changes, but the cause can just as easily be the barista asking you to please wait your turn in line when you inadvertently cut in front of three other people. And you felt blind-sided by her comment. There's practically no limit to the things we may take personally. For the sake of starting at the same trailhead, I compiled some examples you might relate to:

- A friend not pursuing the relationship at the same level you do

- Not being invited to a party or dinner you wanted to attend

- A parent who shows disinterest in your life or criticizes your choices

- Loving someone who doesn't love you back

- A boss who seems to treat you unjustly while other employees get preferential treatment

Can you relate to one or more examples on this list? This list isn't exhaustive, so what would you add to it?

When these things we take personally happen, there's usually a bodily (somatic) reaction, a wave of emotions, and an onslaught of internal Negative Cognitions (NC). My pattern goes like this: *Viscerally*, my heart aches, and my chest feels tight. I'm not present in my heart, mind, or body. I'm overwhelmed by the searing pain of what feels like a personal attack. *Emotionally*, I feel deflated and beaten down, and my ability to be filled with joy and vitality is squelched; there's no song in my heart, no skip in my step. *Internally*, I'm zapped by yet another blow to my heart for what feels like just being me. *It must be me.*

I must be unlovable. They don't love me. My mind races with obsessive thoughts about what they said and what I think they meant. Then I go down the rabbit hole to the pits of despair and the land of confusion.

Through our NCs, we often become storytellers. Let's face it: if we don't have the full picture of a story, we'll make it up. We assign meaning to our visceral and emotional reactions to things others say and do by characterizing them as attacks or digs. And commonly, instead of giving people the benefit of the doubt, we assume they thought the worst of us. To illustrate how this works, I paired the list of examples with sample corresponding NCs:

THINGS WE MAY TAKE PERSONALLY	NEGATIVE COGNITIONS
A friend not pursuing the relationship at the same level you do	I'm too needy, I'm too desperate, I'm annoying
Not being invited to a party or dinner you wanted to attend	I'm not worthy, I'm not enough, I'm unlikable
The parent that shows disinterest in your life or criticizes about your choices	It's never enough, I don't matter, everything I do is wrong
Loving someone who doesn't love you back	I'm unlovable, I'm unworthy, I'm too much, I'm not valuable
The boss who seems to treat you unjustly while other employees get preferential treatment	I'm less-than, I don't deserve respect, I'm invisible

Aside from the heartbreak we suffer when we're disconnected from others, we usually compound that pain by assigning blame to the self. Our heads spin out of control with wild stories behind why they did it, said it, and acted that way. We bury ourselves under the rubble of a narrative that may not be correct and most likely won't serve us or the greater good—not to mention that NC-driven story will keep us spiraling.

The worst part of our explanations is: the stories we make up about how others see us are rarely even close to the truth. When we try to see ourselves through the eyes of others, we tend to presume that we're reading their mind. But we're filling in the blanks by pointing a finger at ourselves. Whatever they said or did that offended us, now we're also finding ourselves guilty and then blaming them for it (this complicates forgiveness, as I discuss later in this chapter). Our evidence is our internal NCs. Consider how this happens to most of us as teenagers, including me. We view our self through a filtered lens of those around us, amplifying every perceived flaw, which can make us self-conscious and sensitive to criticism—and the perception of it. This is a myopic, one-sided view of self and others. Interestingly enough, our impetus toward taking things personally originated as a survival mechanism.

THE ROOT OF TAKING THINGS PERSONALLY

We're humans raised by other humans. What could possibly go wrong?

Absolutely everything, and anything!

We're not at fault for taking things personally. In fact, we have a bent towards negativity that begins in our mother's womb. There, our delicate nervous system already detects circumstances in the environment that feel "off" or unsafe and stores that information for survival. Evolutionarily speaking, our brains are designed to look for patterns of danger and help us avoid them. In prehistoric times, the smartest and most fear-alerted humans survived, thanks to their reptilian brain that looked for any signs of danger. Can we say tiger? For survival, our minds leap to the worst-case scenarios when we hear the proverbial rustling in the brush. The cost of being wrong if you run and then realize there was only a squirrel is much less than the cost of assuming there's a squirrel and then being attacked by a tiger.

There's an almond-shaped fear center in the brain called the "amygdala," which is responsible for our fight-or-flight response to this day. As humans evolved, so have our brains, and we developed more advanced complex systems, namely, the prefrontal cortex, which is responsible for reason, logic, wisdom, and meaning-making. But old patterns die hard, and our amygdala is unaware that times have changed, so it's still ready to launch an attack at the first sign of danger. The amygdala is fully active from birth, whereas the prefrontal cortex develops over the first twenty-five years or so of life.

Through the overprotective amygdala, our brain transforms from the open, creative, loving wiring we're born with to closed-off, judgmental, lonely settings on autopilot. This happens mostly before age seven as our world views take hold and our personality structure develops.

Attachment Theory shows us that we learn our reactions throughout infancy and childhood, developing our "attachment frame," or all elements of our relationship dynamics. These include: interactions between individuals, communication styles, how we navigate and resolve challenges, and other key factors like power dynamics. From an early age, our attachment frames encode information necessary for survival in the amygdala through an "imprinting" process. This happens when, as babies, we were powerless, and our survival depended on the care of others. If our needs weren't met, we blamed ourselves—when we were most blameless—resulting in "scripts" of varying degrees of insecurity, fear, and sometimes paranoia.

So, you can envision how this happens, the following is a very generalized sample of the process:

> The child, being totally dependent on mom and dad for their very survival, has no other choice than to carry the burden of keeping the bond strong. When at times mom and/or dad are upset, frustrated, emotionally withdrawn, absent due to other obligations, and otherwise occupied, the child can't conceptualize that the parent is "bad," or rather, not acting in the best interest of the child by tending to their physical or emotional needs, wherein the child is "good," or rather, that their needs and feelings are fully justified and normal. The attachment frame

sets the child up to flip the script to maintain connection: the child must see themselves as the "bad" one, and mom and dad as "good." To do so, the child must begin to bury vital parts of their being that hold ethos or truth; the energy and authenticity that is their birthright and tells them something is wrong. From this stage on, unless it is corrected, the child will have, somewhere in their being, a part that carries the burden of, "I am unlovable, unworthy, not-enough, too much," etc.

Notice the NCs at the end of the example. They form an imprint script buried in our subconscious that structures our identity and feels like our truth.

When the parent isn't kind to the child, such as being emotionally unavailable, neglectful, or abusive, that child is wired to hate themselves, not the parent. Here's how: As a child our survival depends on holding the connection with our attachment figures (usually mom and dad) and a strong bond with them is paramount to our survival (after all, they are our lifeline), so a child will maintain this bond at any cost, even at the expense of the self. Children are set up to turn an eye inward and bury any parts of the self that may potentially threaten their lifeline, mom and dad. The child has no choice.

Robert Bly explores how we put so much of ourselves into a bag to please our parents in the book, *Meeting the Shadow*. He comments on Alice Miller's *The Drama of the Gifted Child*, writing that:

> We came as infants 'trailing clouds of glory,'
> arriving from the farthest reaches of the
> universe, bringing with us appetites well
> preserved from our mammal inheritance,
> spontaneities wonderfully preserved from
> our 150,000 years of tree life, angers well pre-
> served from our 5000 years of tribal life — in
> short, with our 360 degree-radiance — and we
> offered this gift to parents. They didn't want it.
> They wanted a nice girl or a nice boy.

He explains that parents aren't necessarily terrible here. But they bring us into the world for their reasons, and so did their parents before; those of us who are parents probably do the same to our children. Bly suggests, "Our parents rejected who we were before we could talk, so the pain of rejection is probably stored in some pre-verbal place." Indeed, that place is the psyche, which contains the subconscious and unconscious and communicates with our amygdala beneath our awareness.

You may be like some of my clients and thinking, *but wait, my parents were great. How can you say they rejected me? That my needs weren't met?* This may be true, and yet even those who experienced no physical, verbal, or sexual abuse or neglect sometimes see the manifestations of hidden subconscious agendas wreaking havoc on their relationships in the present. Unable to connect the dots, this can feel confusing and mysterious.

One client shared a story with me about how his mother, whom he adored, was a housewife until he was six years old. Her entire world revolved around him for his whole life. When she told him she was going back to work, he had a meltdown. She did her best to comfort him, being nurturing and present, and she began her new job. That little six-year-old made a vow with himself that day that "Expressing my feelings doesn't matter, so I might as well stuff them down."

Stories like his become lodged deep into some crevice in the psyche, beyond the periphery of consciousness. His imprint illustrates how our frames are constructed when at a young age we experience any sort of injury to the heart and psyche that gets missed by our care-takers and isn't addressed in the moment. In his case, he pushed his hurt down, believing his script's lie that his voice doesn't matter. Years later, as an adult, a be-trayal sent him suffering in the extreme, leading him to seek counseling. Through the therapeutic process, he discovered how his NC led to struggles in adulthood to show vulnerability and connect with others, causing him distress. As often happens, this client realized there was no option but to connect with that injured six-year-old part of himself still calling the shots in his life.

In adulthood, our thoughts, feelings, and behaviors rest in the hands of our nervous system—specifically the amygdala—which transposes our narrative onto other relationships. So, we automatically take things person-ally or feel victimized, launching us into self-analysis, protection, self-blame, and shame, to name a few. *But hold on.* Aren't we supposed to have a mature part of our brain to sort through the nonsense? Not so fast. When the amygdala perceives an old threat, it's activated and overrides the prefrontal cortex—a process dubbed an "amygdala hijack." An NC corresponding to the perceived threat launches, promising imminent death if we don't comply to keep a bond with someone. This explains why, as adults, we will sacrifice a part of ourselves for the sake of connection: like silencing our voice when we should speak up, dimming our creative light so we don't over-power others, and becoming performance-driven, just to name a few.

More often than not, in our modern lives, the an-cient part of our brain misfires, triggering a fight-or-flight response to a non-life-threatening event. Thus, we commonly experience our heart racing and sweaty palms—an adrenaline rush—when we're ghosted for a coffee date or even hear someone else receive praise while we do not. (I'm amazed that the brain still can't differentiate between a perceived threat from a real dan-ger). These amygdala hijackings teach our body and mind to react as if we're in peril—even when we're perfectly safe in our office, maybe just reading an email that gets under our skin.

Our often NC-ladened scripts set us up to needlessly suffer doubly when we take something personally. We judge ourselves, and a secondary layer of pain forms from the assumption others are judging or rejecting us like our early caretakers. This happens when we see ourselves through others' eyes. While judgment of self and other may feel automatic and natural, it's actually a lizard-brain response; one of many other, kinder re-sponses we might choose. You know, like forgiveness of self and the other.

WHY FORGIVENESS "ALONE" DOESN'T WORK

So, you're in the throes of an amygdala hijack. Your NCs are running on repeat, and you're certain the other is judging you the same way. Then, you cool off and let it go. Sometimes. At other times, if you're like me, you want to forgive and forget, but you just... can't.

When faced with a rupture in a relationship, I know firsthand that forgiveness in the name of keeping a connection comes at the expense of my own peace. Of course, it does. Putting a relationship above my feelings is an attachment-based reaction that I learned from my parents; I needed to bury my hurt, sadness, loneliness, and feeling unlovable. Anything to ensure the bond was solid. My well-intentioned parents operated out of their insecurity and fears of rejection and abandonment. They projected a narrative echoing the words they once heard in their families: that forgiving was the right thing to do and to be the bigger person. After all, isn't losing the fight better than losing the friendship? These flimsy messages on forgiveness set me up to dishonor my authentic self, which needed to express my hurt.

Most people learn at a young age that "forgiveness" is the right thing to do, that being able to let go of a grievance is good, to let things slide, to turn a blind eye, and to just "shrug it off." But let's be honest. If we could slough off daggers and just "let it go" that easily, we would be experiencing a different reality, both internally and in the world around us. In the real world, we try to forgive, but it doesn't provide lasting relief for our broken hearts. And we're stuck, unable to move forward. To be clear, I don't think forgiveness isn't necessary, just that it is insufficient if additional necessary steps haven't been met first.

We can't just forgive and move on because our hearts know the well-meaning advice and all those sermons aren't sufficient. Rushing to forgive means we're trying to extend a divine act toward another. . . while we desperately need that energy and focus to heal our pain first. So, we're bypassing the steps necessary to forgive, and then we remain upset, feeling intensely ashamed that we're somehow flawed because we can't "forgive others as God forgives us." That advice the church proclaims wounds our souls with confusion and frustration, which our hearts and minds can't reconcile. After all, how can there be peace without justice? *There can't be.*

So, why do we rush to forgive when that doesn't work? There's a name for it: "spiritual bypass." John Welwood describes this as "A tendency to use spiritual ideas and practices to sidestep or avoid facing unresolved emotional issues, psychological wounds, and unfinished developmental tasks." If you grew up in a church where the message of forgiveness is handed out as easily and quickly as the program when you enter services, you may have learned to spiritually bypass necessary healing work. Perhaps, when we struggle to forgive, instead of feeling unworthy of grace, we can slow down and cultivate it.

THE MIND AND BODY INTERCONNECTED

The amygdala teaches the mind *and* body how to react in situations deemed life-or-death. Because in learning what counts as threatening, our brains encode conflict with caretakers as our fault, but how does the body factor into taking things personally? To discover why and how old emotions stick with our minds and bodies, we must consider the interrelations between our neurological, biological, and psychological levels.

Perhaps you've heard of the body-mind split, an idea that a French philosopher from the 17th century, Rene Descartes, is credited for discovering. Most people today believe this to be true. I might agree, if not for my philosophy professor, Dr. Levinson. He once said, "You can't separate the mind and the body." Decades later, these words mean more to me than they ever have. When the mind is distressed, so is the body (and vice versa). We don't need to be under extraordinary stress for the body to suffer if our minds are suffering. Perhaps you've felt this connection and maybe even put two and two together, like how worrying can cause stomach pain or lead to ulcers. More subtly, a looming deadline may trigger tightness in the neck. Many such connections exist between our feelings and our physical pains or ailments.

Eastern medicine, with its 5000 years of proven principles, supports modern medicine to show how our emotions significantly impact our bodies. A friend of mine discovered this in a consultation with an acupuncturist a few months after having back surgery. As the doctor examined her back, he asked, with great concern, what happened to her. She reminded him of her recent surgery.

He said, "I mean a long time ago and over a long period of time."

"Oh, you must mean the beatings," she said. He told

her she was covered in emotional papercuts, so she disclosed childhood verbal and physical abuse, which she usually shared with mental health providers, not her medical team. But Eastern medicine is holistic and understands that when we experience heartbreak and are unable to release the upset, our hearts and bodies constrict, demonstrating a direct and powerful link between the heart, body, and mind. In treating her back pain, her back released tension through Chinese herbs and techniques as she processed emotions she'd stuffed down to survive as a child. Until we first connect with the mind and its stories and emotions, we will feel the impact in the body and carry it with us.

Western medicine is slowly acknowledging the link between our inner worlds, that whole realm of emotions, and our bodies. In the New York Times bestselling book, *The Body Keeps the Score: Brain, Mind, and Body in the Healing of Trauma*, Dutch psychiatrist and author Bessel A. van der Kolk explains that:

> . . . trauma is much more than a story about something that happened long ago. The emotions and physical sensations that were imprinted during the trauma are experienced not as memories but as disruptive physical reactions in the present.

Therefore, physical distress, particularly when we're in emotional turmoil, can be your body pointing you toward a past hurt. Ever have the proverbial wind knocked out of you when something reminds you of a long-buried painful event from your past? And you physically feel like it's happening all over again? Then, a script pipes up to explain what's wrong, and once again, you judge yourself and judge yourself through the lens of the other. The past becomes the present.

Now that we have a full picture of why we take things personally and why we hold onto them, there is hope of changing our reactions. Van der Kolk explains that somatic healing arrives when we ". . . reset [our] physiology" so the body "stops working against [us]." Osteopathic Medicine teaches that the body's natural state is health, and it always wants to return to that state. So, why would the body hurt us? The answer is simple. Like any pain signal, it points to something that needs your attention to heal. When we fail to heed this beckoning, it will come out, as I call it, "sideways" in the form of addictions, self-contempt, rage, shame, and other unhelpful coping mechanisms. The body may also express "sideways" pleas, such as headaches when you're going to see a certain relative.

The unconscious will beckon us until its needs and longings are met. In the meantime, it holds onto the pain in our heart and soul, making forgiveness fleeting at best. In the next chapter, I further explore what happens in the psyche when we take things personally and why only a holistic approach can truly free us of our grievances.

POINTS OF CONTEMPLATION

Ready to open up to the possibility that there's a lot more going on beneath the waterline when it comes to taking things personally? Respond to the following questions to begin noticing the invisible forces at work when you've struggled to let things go.

- Notice how the roots of taking things personally apply to your personal story. What are some things you've taken personally? List 3-5 and write down the NCs that flashed through your mind for each.

- Describe a situation when you rushed to forgive to keep the peace or hold the connection in a relationship. What happened in the end? How did that make you feel?

- What's a time when you felt guilt or shame that you weren't able to forgive someone? What did you do to try and forgive? What step was missing?

- Consider when you felt constrictions in the body connected to an emotional disturbance. What was that sensation? Where did you feel it?

CHAPTER 2

The Only Way
Out is Through

"The wound is the place where the light enters you"

—RUMI

Have you ever been swept up in a conversation with a friend, processing how you were hurt, victimized, or wronged? In those moments, we're looking to have our feelings validated and our pain alleviated. There's nothing wrong with feeling hurt, expressing what's in our hearts, and receiving comfort from a trusted confidante. However, when we take things personally, we may not leave those conversations healed, experiencing a long-lasting calm that stands the test of time. Instead, we rather quickly revert to our NCs, stewing in our frustration. That well-intended advice doesn't stick to our hearts and souls as we hoped. We remain unsettled, and our grudges continue to impact our mind and body, as well as our heart and soul.

That has been my experience with many strategies to let things go. I was told that writing all the many blessings I should be thankful for in my gratitude journal would improve my mood. I have attended workshops on compassion, listened to self-improvement podcasts, gone on yoga retreats, done breathwork, and seen several therapists who listened and validated my story - all to help me relieve the heaviness I still feel from NCs imprinted when I was on the receiving end of injustices that happened years ago.

I've also tried to talk myself out of feeling upset. After all, my life is pretty good, and circumstances could be much worse for me. For that, I *am* grateful. Yet, I'm upset again *every* time I think of what happened. Can you relate to this all-too-common journey of seeking peace and enlightenment, just to have it elude you at every turn? Over the years, clients have poured their hearts out lamenting the hurts they haven't been able to reconcile and sharing the list of the antidotes they tried in hopes they would resolve the pain, but to no avail.

We eventually seek help from experts such as therapists. While well-intentioned, they may give us a diagnosis instead of a road map out of the pain. Not because they don't care, but because diagnosing is what they're trained to do. The DSM5, which is a thick diagnostic manual used by mental health providers, is filled with codes and descriptions of every psychopathology known to man. Clinicians use this manual to give patients a label, which essentially describes how their mental state is creating behaviors that don't serve them and are impacting the individual in unhealthy, dysfunctional, and negative ways--such as Intermittent Explosive Disorder (anger), Cluster Personality Disorder (social awkwardness and withdrawal), and Substance Abuse Disorder (addictions) are just a few–with deleterious consequences. Labels aren't tools to heal the human heart with all its longings and unmet needs, nor do diagnoses describe how to improve communication and connection in relationships.

I believe the majority of mental health diagnoses in the DSM5 are a result of our instinctively building walls of protection from the supposed enemy, inadvertently imprisoning ourselves from being free to love others as well. Doing so, we become disconnected from love—the most powerful energy that flows through the universe. As psychiatrist and author Curt Thompson points out, "All psychological and emotional problems are rooted in the inability to receive love." Without it, we become abbreviated versions of ourselves; fragmented and lost, our hearts darken, at the most extreme like Ebeneezer Scrooge or Darth Vader. Even if we don't become full-on villains, a shadow in our hearts eclipses the light and projects itself onto others and ourselves.

We're searching for something out there to soothe our discomfort—when perhaps. . . just maybe, some of us are preventing love from reaching us. The heart knows if this is true, and in its infinite wisdom, it will not settle for cheap substitutes. We need to listen to that wisdom. The only way out of our heartaches is through them, which is how we restore our flow of love. At the end of this chapter, you'll find an overview of the Never Personal Process, which leads to the birdseye view where we see that it was never personal.

MATTERS OF THE HEART

The "flow of love" can be a heady concept. You might think of the flow of love like a river, and its current can be jammed up by too many fallen leaves. They prevent the river from flowing naturally in the same way that things we take personally limit the flow of love to and through us. And we restore our healthy flow by removing judgment of ourselves and others.

Here's an example of love flowing through us that might be familiar to you: You receive a call from one of your children or your best friend; you hear their voice, and your heart lights up with joy. You beam with pride at how much you appreciate their presence in your life and how well you have maintained a solid, healthy relationship with them. Whatever their reason for calling, you adorn them with words of praise and talk in the softest, most supportive, sweetest voice possible. You aim to be loving and responsive. As you hang up, your heart continues to bask in the lingering good vibes over the connection of love that you feel with them.

Life is good; this is feeling fully alive and connected with our fellow humans. After all, we are wired for connection. That's what healthy attachment frames do. Loving people and enjoying all the benefits of our connections often feels easy, like water flowing downstream. We can enjoy relationships absent of messages from the past.

Then, you go to lunch with your close friend, Erin. You're enjoying a light-hearted, casual conversation, then she scowls. It slides across her face almost out of nowhere as she describes a mutual friend (someone who has been nothing but kind to her for over 30 years and who she never had a cross word with), and there it is; the truth of how Erin truly feels about the other in the deepest champers of her heart. The distaste in her voice sends chills through you—an immediate somatic disturbance in your heart. She utters, "I don't think she's really as nice as she tries to come off as being. I think she's a fake. What do you think about her?" Erin pauses, and disgust clings to her face. You dart your eyes away, now knowing she's capable of turning around (perhaps even right after lunch) and saying the same thing about you. While she has every right to her feelings, you're witnessing a shadowy side of Erin, and instead of drawing you toward her with a confidence, she's pushing you away.

The heart isn't built to tear one person down and also genuinely build another up. This isn't about pointing the finger or setting out to find the bad guy, but Erin's flow of love to you is reduced by her walls with the other friend, which constrict her heart. Until she addresses that, she'll approach her relationships with a veneer of sweetness that prevents genuine emotional intimacy.

We can be fooled into thinking all our interpersonal relationships are running on full throttle when our hearts are wide open for one person—whether it be our partners, our children, our business associates, or even the guy serving bagels at the local breakfast joint—but closed off to others (i.e. the friend you harbor feelings of contempt for because you believe she is fake). In this dichotomy, we often don't realize that the ones we're sharing our "heart wide open" with only receive a slow trickle of our love.

The human heart is designed in such a uniquely beautiful way that doors closed for one (the homeless man who seems to have fallen out of grace years ago and that you ignore every time you walk by) mean doors are closed for all. We can't effectively build one person up (our children, spouses, family) while dismissing, disgracing, or disrespecting another. Everyone loses.

Jesus reminds us of this principle in Matthew 25:40 when he says, "Truly, I say to you, as you did it to one of the least of these my brothers, you did it to me." That scripture is commonly understood about outward behavior, but its meaning extends into the heart's unseen layers—the hidden ones that come out sideways as comments seep out, revealing our true feelings. The Quran expresses a similar concept in Verses 5:32–33: "If anyone kills a person, it would be as if he killed the whole people: and if anyone saved a life, it would be as if he saved the life of the whole people." We're deceiving ourselves if we think we can be cruel, greedy, unfriendly, rejecting, or hateful to one person and sequester another part of our heart for being kind to others.

OUR PLACE IN THE UNIVERSE

The flow of love is one aspect of the universal flow of energy that runs through all of existence. Many faith traditions, including Christianity, Buddhism, Judaism, Islam, and Hinduism, view the universal flow as our connection to God, universal consciousness, Source, and spiritual interconnection with all things. We come into the world like any living being, completely embodying the energy and fullness of our purpose; we are conduits for the energy that pulsates throughout the entire universe to move through us and into creation. We are creative beings, designed to flourish and become the best versions of ourselves. Like how in nature, a flower or tree grows to the fullest, most abundant version of itself when given the right conditions: proper soil, light, and water. We are no different.

However, in conditions that thwart growth and bend the natural flow of things, we become spiritually and psychologically crippled versions of ourselves. That happens like a grape that gets too much sun and not enough water withers on the vine. Poor conditions are constrictions in our scripts from betrayals, fear, grief, loss, and limiting beliefs. Simply put, when we have knee-jerk reactions or focus on all the bad things someone has done (and why we imagine they did that hurtful thing) instead of putting our energy toward something constructive and life-affirming, the redirected energy misguides our purpose.

Although Eastern Medicine understood flow or Qi for over 2,000 years, psychologist Mihaly Csikszentmihalyi introduced the concept to modern psychology in the late 20th century. In his book, *Flow: The Psychology of Optimal Experience,* He describes psychic energy generated by our nervous systems that structures our consciousness, which endlessly flows when ". . . attention can be freely invested to achieve a person's goals because there is no disorder to straighten out, no threat for the self to defend against." Csikszentmihalyi argues that while in a flow state, we express ourselves and our purpose authentically, and out of flow, we're inauthentic and controlled by society, self-criticism, and fear of judgment.

Consider how naturally most children inhabit this space of freedom and expression; just watch them on the playground or with some crayons and a blank canvas. Their creativity is effortless. Likewise, in a flow state, we're one with the universe, collaborating to manifest art in all its forms—be that problem-solving or quilting, architecture or water polo. In *The Artist's Way: A Spiritual Path to Higher Creativity*, Julia Cameron writes.

> ... think of the universe as a vast electrical sea in which you are immersed and from which you are formed, opening your creativity changes you from something bobbing in that sea to a more fully functioning, more conscious, more cooperative part of that ecosystem... [triggering] *synchronicity*: we change, and the universe furthers and expands that change.

Thus, access to our energetic flow aligns our creativity and effectiveness with the world around us. That harmony is collateral damage when we take things personally. In the fallout of being unable to forgive, our energetic flow is constricted, bringing even more pain, confusion, and self-judgment because we feel unable to make a difference. We may waste our energy on tearing others down and focusing on the negative in our lives.

I found myself out of flow last week during my piano lesson. I take piano lessons from a brilliant instructor, Brad, a classically trained pianist. He and his wife have a conservatory with two grand pianos in their lovely, historic home. During my most recent lesson, I played him a song I had been practicing for some time, "Sunset in Madrid," knowing there was room for much improvement: coordinating both hands and the timing of the pedal is no easy thing! As I played the song, anxiety coursed through my body, and I stiffened. The timing of the pedaling was off. I thought, *Whoa. Holy cow. He must think I suck.* Then, I imagined his voice in my head, saying, *She sure is stupid. I expected her to be further along.*

Later in the session, his wife entered the room. In my usual default mode, when I'm insecure and believe others are judging me, I rush in and beat them to the punch. So, in my usual manner of exiting out of my discomfort, I blurted out, "Sorry you must listen to this. At least Brad's getting paid." We all enjoyed a good laugh.

Upon reflection, I noticed how my self-critic has perfected this move for decades: I'm going to get me before you get me! That's a preemptive strike against the self. What would it have cost me to stay present in the discomfort? I would've had to wrestle with the part of myself holding the vulnerable feeling of not being good enough—the place where growth occurs when we break through barriers and allow creativity to flow.

After I finished performing the piece, he said, in his gentle and kind manner, "I don't think it's helping you when you talk to yourself negatively like that. I think it's damaging your progress."

Grievances against ourselves and others can rob us of our creative expression and our authentic nature, turning us into people we're not meant to be and sending us down lonely paths we don't want to take. This can happen in small ways, like how my NC made it difficult for me to stay present, in the flow, and pour heart and soul into the piece I was playing. Had I not been in self-protection mode, I would have had freed-up energy to play the song and maybe surprised myself and Brad. However, left unchecked, my inner critic's hurtful words—and those I imagined my teacher thinking—could've snowballed such that I stopped practicing, quit lessons, and even sold my piano, never to play again!

Have you experienced how self-judgments stay lodged in the psyche and dictate areas of your life? The impact can happen in big ways, too: not marrying someone you love because you feel unworthy; always wanting to play the flute but never picking one up for fear of failure; and avoiding being seen because you feel unattractive. Those are a small sample of the invisible ways constricted energy diminishes our lives beyond the pain of taking things personally.

THE NEVER PERSONAL PROCESS

Fortunately, we can restore our spiritual and energetic connection; to do so, we must address the wrongs we're holding onto and lower the walls around our hearts. This process begins with flipping the script on our NCs. *No biggie, right?* In my life, feeling "unlovable" has caused me to take things personally in many extraordinarily painful ways, like parents who at times didn't show up for me emotionally the way I needed them to, lovers who acted in ways that left me feeling rejected, friends who excluded me from social gatherings, colleagues who nearly succeeded in blemishing my character. My life story provided mounting evidence that, at the core, I was unlovable and alone in this world. Sure, we've heard how this is a cruel, lonely world, taking no prisoners. But this felt personal to me. I sometimes thought, *Others can't have possibly suffered the same blows I have.* Others in my social circle didn't seem burdened with the heaviness of feeling that they are not-enough or too much. At times, I lamented my suffering.

After I took the steps that eventually comprised my Never Personal Process (NPP), my visual acuity increased. Seeing my past more clearly, I delved into the originating memory for the "I am unlovable" imprint. There, in that very network of scripts, I found the place of power for me to begin rewriting that narrative with a new view of self and others. Misdirected energy, once expended into being judgmental towards others and myself, now had a precise focus to generate productive thoughts and actions.

With my newfound clarity, I saw that many others were also suffering and felt stuck because of these same kinds of past scripts that lead us to take things personally well into adulthood. Here's a quick recap: Our developing selves needed to take things personally to survive, but now those imprints hijack our relationships with others and ourselves. Perhaps you, too, have been heavy-hearted over being on the receiving end of an offense, convinced that "it must be me." Thoughts of "why me" lead to assumptions of what the offending parties think of me. Essentially, we turn a critical eye toward the self. We vacillate between being on the defensive to protect ourselves and trying to people please and curry favor. Or we can flip the script.

Our unnecessary suffering in taking things personally resides in old scripts handed to us as our brains were developing, and we began to play our part. The victim. However, we have the power to rewrite our NCs and move ourselves from the viewpoint of being "acted upon" to the birdseye view in which it was never personal. I invite you to walk this five-step Never Personal Process with me through the rest of the book.

1. Identify the Raw Spot: Intercept an amygdala hijacking and consider what happened when you first felt hurt like you feel now. There, you'll find the roots of what you're taking personally.

2. Hold and Release: Listen for the NC to uncover the painful emotions you avoided feeling years ago. In doing so, soothe the ache to clear it from your mind and body.

3. Integrating the Whole / View of Self: Look for new information or different perspectives to draw contrasts between your hurt feelings in the present and those in the past. This shifts the effect this past situation has on you from a self-focus to a more objective focus.

4. Widening the Lens / View of the Other: Forgiveness becomes realistic because you now have the capacity for compassion and discerning a redemptive script that honors the self and the other. Appropriate boundaries can be set.

5. Birdseye View: Complete the journey from blaming ourselves and others to removing blame from the equation through adopting a non-binary lens. This physically and psychologically brings us to realize that it was never personal.

The following chapters walk you through these steps so you can repeat them any time you feel yourself taking something personally. The NPP is linear in nature, but not necessarily in practice. You may find latitude in the healing journey to take one step forward and then two steps back. However, the first step is always the same. In Chapter 3, you'll learn to identify the raw spots, getting to the root of why we really feel so hurt in the present, when we can heal our pain from the past.

POINTS OF CONTEMPLATION

Resist any urges to judge the Never Personal Process or the self. Give yourself permission to suspend your criticism, replacing it with curiosity: What might it mean for you if this is true? The following questions will help you sift through potential resistance and notice when you've seen elements of the process play out in your experience.

- When did you or someone you loved sought mental health support for an emotional upset and received a diagnosis? Did that lead to healing or peace? Why or why not?

- What's a time that you loved one person while withholding love from another? How did that feel in your heart? What happened with the relationship you were trying to build?

- Have you experienced someone tearing another down, while trying to love you or someone else well? How did you know? Did it seem to work?

- Recall a time when self-criticism took you out of a present moment. What was the result? What might have been possible if you hadn't felt constricted?

CHAPTER 3

Identify Your Raw Spots

*"Knowing others is intelligence, knowing
yourself is true wisdom."*

—LAOZI

If doling out forgiveness was as easy as just "letting
stuff go," there probably wouldn't be so much human
suffering over lingering grievances. But there is. And
plenty of it stems from incidents in which we were
mistreated or victimized. One client was especially burdened with overwhelming feelings of guilt and shame
from not being able to forgive her perpetrator, a high
school science teacher, for horrific acts when she was
a vulnerable sixteen-year-old. Undoubtedly, she was a
victim in that story, and she took his actions personally.

When he betrayed her trust, unbeknownst to her,
an emotional and psychological wound was inflicted,
which would then be covered up by an adulthood
spent pretending she was okay. She had heard all the
sermons on forgiveness, attended bible studies on the
importance of extending compassion to others, read
Bible verses repeatedly on how God forgives us, and

believed good spiritual hygiene involves extending that to others. Of course, she also performed her daily rosary bead morning ritual—all in the hopes of experiencing peace in the furthest depths of her being. Yet she remained unable to shake the revulsion that came up at the mere thought of that man.

Now in her fifties, this client was still wallowing in a sea of constriction, hurt, resentment, bitterness, and shame; all of which were compounded by her confusion over why she wasn't able to "just forgive" as her pastor instructed her to do (and assured her it would lead to freedom!). The burning question, *What's wrong with me?*, rattled around in her brain. Isn't something wrong with us when we're unable to just forgive in the face of an offense—especially because we know doing so would feel so much better? She brought these questions to my office hoping to glean anything she might've overlooked on her quest for forgiveness and redemption.

Like so many, she unknowingly bypassed the first necessary step toward forgiveness. She needed to connect with a *raw spot* in all its tenderness and nurture it in a way that honored her. Raw spots are the part of our being that carries hurts we buried in our developmental years to please our caretakers, forming our attachment frames. They contain the NCs and scripts that blamed us when we were blameless. By doing the work outlined in this chapter, she laser-focused on the place where she was holding that wound. It imprinted a script that what happened was her fault for a whole host of NCs. After unburdening herself of those lies, she freed herself to leave the incident in her past.

I share this example to illustrate how even when we have clarity that someone else behaved wrongly, we can't just move on because somewhere in our psyche, there's a raw spot holding self-blame. It's linked with a network of scripts within our attachment frame. Thus, letting go of grudges when we're hurt by someone else isn't a straight path for most of us. We better understand forgiveness by approaching it slowly. The first step is tracing the subconscious source of why we may think others are wronging us—because they believe our NCs. In this chapter, we'll look at how to access our raw spots and deal with the past to finally rid ourselves of pain.

PARTS OF OUR IDENTITIES

Have you ever ridden a horse? I've heard of horseback riding as a metaphor for the tug-of-war between our conscious and subconscious minds. The rider is the conscious mind holding the reins to steer our intentions, plans, and goals. The horse stands for the unconscious mind and its parts, agendas, and driving forces that impact our behavior, which sometimes may seem irrational. Here's a story to illustrate: Many years ago, on a sunny afternoon, a high school friend and I were riding horses. I believed that I was the rider in control. We took off from the stables, and at some point, my horse decided to turn around and take off back to the barn. My grip wasn't strong enough, but through my cleverness and willpower, I decided to direct that horse back to where I wanted us to go. However, the horse maintained all the power and dictated our course, regardless of my desires to the contrary. That day, I, the rider, was powerless.

We do well to respect the balance of power between our conscious and subconscious selves. The latter often contains our raw spots with all their NCs, tucked beyond the periphery of our conscious minds, making up our complex personality structure. While people generally believe we govern ourselves with our rational minds, making choices and taking actions by exercising free will (If that were so, then we could simply decide not to feel emotional pain), we're often highjacked by our internal, subconscious system and subject to its whims.

In Chapter 1, you learned about the roots of our scripts and the overprotective amygdala. Our beautifully complex personalities were not created in a vacuum. In the field of psychology we see that as the child experiences their environment, ego states (sometimes referred to as "parts") begin to develop, constructing the child's view of self and view of others. These parts are frozen in time and hold stories of who we "think" we are, which impact how we view ourselves and others in adulthood.

Consider my client who felt rejected as a child and created a script around it of being not-enough (one part), then over-performing in school (another part), and has a self-critic (another part) that keeps a tight grip on everything they could be doing wrong to fix it, reinforcing guardrails which serve to hold connection and avoid rejection. Some of those parts contain vulnerable raw spots that hold an emotional charge and their accompanying NCs, glomming onto our psyches and having their way with them.

When working with clients, we map out the rigid structure of their identity and peel back layers. There, we find raw spots with roots in an earlier time when someone said or did something to them that caused an NC to imprint upon them. For me, it was that I was unlovable, and other times not-enough. Later in life, this imprint served as a template through which I ran every scene and assigned meanings to others' words and actions. I was astonished to learn in *A Course of Miracles* that when I took something personally, I believed my internal experience of feeling hurt was happening outside of me, in the world. But actually, we experience external events and then internally ascribe meaning to them. Since that meaning can be based on outdated scripts and imprints, we can judge someone for wronging us and feel a need to forgive them just because our ego is wounded, with no basis on current facts and realities.

For instance, if my client's not-enough part feels implicated when they're fired, those hurt feelings could obfuscate the truth that 90% of their department was cut, and the decision couldn't have been more impersonal. Now, on top of practical job-hunting concerns, their raw spots are bubbling to the surface, forcing them to reckon with why they were lacking in some way. The client could be sucked into that dark alley, or they could take a step back and notice what's really happening, versus what are meanings they're making and why.

If you feel offended, say, maybe someone doesn't include you, even though you know you're frequently invited to events and have many friends, you may feel that emotional reaction was beneath you. But this hurt feeling makes sense when we ask, "What happened to me when I learned this script?" versus "What's wrong with me?" The first question can show you a raw spot, like a time your older siblings were doing something together you were too small to do, and you learned an NC that you're not-enough to be included. The second question implies a negative connotation with "wrong" straight out the gate. Judgment rarely lands us any place good—or where we would like to be. The more we wonder where a hurt feeling comes from when it arises, the better we understand "why" we interpret our experiences the way we do—and take some things personally.

NOT GETTING STUCK IN THE MUCK

Some readers may wonder if delving into our raw spots is actually necessary, especially if you've heard new-age thinkers argue you only need to "be present" and think positively. They say there's no value in revisiting the past because it's like playing the same old tapes on repeat. Can't we just get out of Dodge? Okay, at first, the "moving on" reasoning seems to make perfect sense; we don't want to stay stuck in the muck. However, moving on in the healing journey without holding and releasing keeps you stuck in the same narrative because you want to forgive—but are unable to. While re-wiring the mind is a piece of the Never Personal Process, if the inner child isn't heard, the attachment wound remains in the unconscious and holds onto the NC; and without the somatic piece, the body still carries that memory. That often leaves people with more questions than answers because your raw spot still feels too raw, and it needs tending to. It's still *painful*. . . so you stay stuck.

And no wonder. The restoration of buried wounds requires a holistic approach. So many therapies, modalities, and spiritual principles don't fully reach the depths of the crevices where our pain resides—where corrective emotional experiences take place. That's because these solutions don't access all parts of the individual that withstood the shock of the original wound. For instance, Cognitive Behavioral Therapy (CBT) often avoids underlying emotional issues and integration of self and body, and A Course in Miracles addresses the ego without the somatic work.

Whether it be tried and true modalities or emerging ones with fresh labels and added tweaks to old standards, the vital thing to remember is that the most complete path toward healing includes our psychological, somatic, and spiritual pieces. John Pierrakos characterizes this process as:

> A person who goes into spirituality without having worked out his negativities – his ego defenses, his resistances – flies high like Icarus, but when he reaches the burning sun, he falls into the sea the sea of life and drowns. It is only through transcending and working through the obstacles to life that the human being can rise into realms of creation and spirituality.

Many aspects of our being are disrupted by the blows and injustices of this world, so we must tap into our multi-layers to connect these pieces of ourselves (all bundled into one body) with a raw spot submerged in the psyche. The raw spot's beauty and power is that we have access to all those mentioned above to move to the next step of flipping the script.

WHY DEALING WITH THE PAST MATTERS TODAY

Excavating the past by combing through our history can feel daunting, like irrelevant navel gazing or unrelated to events in your life today. But as astronomer Carl Sagan famously said, "You have to know the past to understand the present." The goal is to trace our past to the raw spots embedded in the unconscious. Through understanding how our identities formed, we come to grasp the original wounds that inform our belief systems, influence our behaviors, and seem to powerfully rule our emotions.

Those raw spots remain raw because they're unresolved within the subconscious. There, we carry emotions that were too difficult to fully feel at the time, and when we try to 'just move on,' we bring those emotions with us. The ties that bind us to the past are very real at this stage of healing. However, unearthing the root of our pain allows us to meet longings and unmet needs buried in this part of your identity. Sounds like a lot of work, right? Well, *yes, a lot of inner work is wrapped up in this bundle, beckoning us to revisit the past. Yet, all our efforts to bypass the higher road (towards peace) will only lead to delayed healing, frustration, and oftentimes confusion.*

Bypassing any stage of healing is unlikely to achieve the results we long for.

Unacknowledged raw spots from the past are like shackles that bind our joy and creative expression in the present, as they restrict our access to the universal flow. I've heard it said that "the only sins that imprison us are the ones we're unaware of." Given this, looking into our past is a worthwhile journey. Doing so sets us free. We're no longer captives to our raw spots and their flawed scripts about who we are and what's true for us. As if we need more reasons to be motivated to connect with and heal the past, author Walter Wangerin offers a profound message for us to contemplate:

> There are 2 different types of people in the world, those who know what their insecurities are, and those who do not. And the ones who do not are the most dangerous people in the world.

The flipside is, the better in touch we are with our insecurities imprinted into our scripts, the less likely we are to hurt ourselves and others—intentionally or otherwise.

Indeed, the consequences of not dealing with our past reach into the crevices of our lives in ways we rarely imagined possible. Like smoke from a fire, the past cannot be hidden. It's unrelenting in its beckoning for us to visit, and those invitations come in the forms of alcoholism, anger, sarcasm, self-contempt, and any number of defense mechanisms. Those are manifestations of the raw spot's energy calling out for us to pay attention to it. Our unresolved feelings (which originate in the self-blame we learned as children to protect our bonds with caretakers) tend to come out sideways in our relationships with others, God, and self.

The past will stop at nothing in its relentless pursuit to turn our attention toward what needs to be healed. This urgency often stems from a surprising reveal: *So much of the past connects with our present story.* The heaviness of NCs begins to lift as we gain an awareness of how our experiences have impacted our behaviors.

For example, perhaps as a child, you learned to play quietly to please your grandmother, and now with your children, their loudness inexplicably sparks your fury—but why? They're happily playing, and you believe their expressions are healthy. Yet you're running a script where yelling is forbidden and gets you sent to the "bad corner." Beneath that memory, you were humiliated by your grandmother's rejection of your peals of glee (even if, granted, you might've been a little annoying). By identifying and tending to that raw spot, your conscious and subconscious mind won't pull against each other, so you can parent with your adult mind, not your reactive five-year-old self.

Self-awareness of how our early experiences shape our reactions to present events lays the groundwork for accepting our long-buried difficult truths. The mystery is shattered. Dealing with the past opens a pathway for longing and pain to lift as we grieve losses and wounds we were unable to before.

TENDING THE RAW SPOTS

While the human heart wasn't designed to withstand the shattering blows of betrayals and rejection, science has gifted us with a safety valve to release ourselves from the pain and despair of taking things personally. Nothing, and I mean nothing, will change or heal a human heart other than what we call a corrective emotional experience in psychology. This requires connecting with the raw spot that was wounded at the time of the offense and revisiting that wound in the present. I break that process down over the following two chapters. To create a corrective emotional experience, we must first locate the raw spot. It, along with its fallout, didn't just leave a raw spot on the heart, a distortion in the mind, and a bend in the spirit; it created a ding to the nervous system that also needs to be tended to. All these factors leave a trail we can follow right back to the source.

Several therapeutic modalities offer strategies for connecting parts of us from the past holding raw spots (emotional charges) and bringing them new information. Richard Schwartz describes this process as Internal Family Systems (IFS) in *No Bad Parts*; he aims to update the script—like updating a smartphone app. The point is to engage our parts to detect emotional wounds from the past that need to be excavated, faced, and healed. Similarly, Eye Movement Desensitization and Reprocessing (EMDR) is a method to rejoin the left and right sides of the brain (one holding the logic, reason, and wisdom, the other the memory and emotional charge) and revisit the past. There, we process and reduce the emotional intensity of the trauma; we can further weave in Ego State Therapy, founded by John and Helen Watkins, to promote healing. Yet another is EFIT (Emotionally Focused Individual Therapy), which helps individuals melt rigid emotional patterns by clearing the ego states around the primary emotions of raw spots: sadness, shame, and fear. These therapeutic modalities are a sample of many emerging techniques shaping modern therapy practices.

Here's an overview of my process, which draws inspiration from several modalities: With clients, we begin investigating the current hurt and its accompanying script as "triggering events." We try to pinpoint what happened to trigger, or activate, the amygdala and the NC that came up to explain the threat. I often use the image of the trigger as a launch pad for exploring the parts of the self that feel under threat. The process involves accessing all aspects of the trigger they can recall—visual pictures, emotions, and somatic sensations. With those details, we explore related ego states, leading to the moment of imprint.

I ask them to float back to a moment when they felt this all too familiar feeling. For example, I might ask, "At what age do you recall first feeling this sadness?" Then, we allow the mind to take us where it needs to complete this excavation. Sometimes, we address an ego state Carl Jung dubbed the "inner child." This is the part of the self still frozen in the painful memory, not knowing time has moved on, and now you're a safe, strong adult. Once we arrive at the origin, we bring the raw spot stuck in childhood new insights and clarity from the adult self.

To illustrate how this plays out, here's a common

pattern; a client seeks help because they were dumped, and now their heart is pummeled. They might have an NC around not-enough, accompanied by a litany of things they did wrong and what they'll do or not do to avoid ever feeling this way again. Then we go back to the moment their feelings were hurt. What exactly was said or done that set their emotions into an uproar? The ego states emerge, and a battle between their perfectionist and inner critic parts unfolds. In teasing these parts out, we rewind to when the client recalls first feeling rejected as a child. We're not always looking for a specific memory, although it's fine if various images and memories come to mind.

The pain an inner child kept a lid on can be breath-taking. So painful that for the rest of their life up to this point, hiding the raw spot in the subconscious and beating themselves up seemed safer than tending the wound. Once it's identified, we can trust the mind to lead us down the necessary path to begin connecting the dots and allow healing.

The benefit of taking the journey within goes far beyond our personal growth, healing, and fulfillment, as it reaches into the lives of others as well, allowing them to benefit. Instead of becoming hoarders of our personal stories of suffering and redemption, we free ourselves up to offer them as gifts to others who are not as far along in the process. Consider Maya Angelou's wisdom in her autobiography, *I Know Why the Caged Bird Sings*. As a 7-yr old girl Black girl in the Jim Crow era South, she is raped and stops speaking. Her story and desire for freedom are caged inside her because she feels like a victim, powerless. As she starts speaking again, she expresses herself with a song of hope loud enough that others may hear it and be inspired. Almost 50 years after its publication, this book was cited as foundational to the #metoo movement. Exploration is a gift to self and others.

POINTS OF CONTEMPLATION

Consider if there's a tender/raw place within you. What if connecting to this part of yourself is the beginning of finding peace from taking things personally? Answer the following questions to find clues that may help you identify some raw spots. For any topics that feel emotionally unsafe, perhaps wait and explore those with a skilled trauma therapist.

- List some situations when an emotion hijacked you.

- For each item you listed, how did you feel at the moment? What did you do? How did you feel about your response later?

- What are some painful events from your past that you tried to ignore and rise above? What happened in the short term? Long term?

- Once you identify a raw spot, allow yourself to float back to a time in your life when this felt like it became a part of your identity. What NB did it teach you? How has that affected your relationships and life choices?

CHAPTER 4

Hold and Release

There was a man who was so disturbed by the sight of his own shadow and so displeased with his own footsteps, that he determined to get rid of both.

The method he hit upon was to run away from them.

So he got up and ran.

But every time he put his foot down there was another step, while his shadow kept up with him without the slightest difficulty.

He attributed his failure to the fact that he was not running fast enough.

So he ran faster and faster, without stopping, until he finally dropped dead.

He failed to realize that if he merely stepped into the shade, his shadow would vanish, and if he sat down and stayed still, there would be no more footsteps.

—CHUANG TZU

From *The Way of Chuang Tzu* (translated/ interpreted by Thomas Merton)

Wisdom teachers throughout the ages, from Jesus to Lao Tzu (and too many psychology gurus to list), point toward the value of handling and connecting with our emotions in a healthy manner—specifically, creating a harmonious relationship with our raw spots. To achieve this inner peace, *We must first hold that which we need to release.* What a simplistic yet powerful way to summarize a great truth central to psychology, philosophy, and spirituality, which has proven to be a necessary step on the journey of realizing that "it" was never personal.

The job of holding and releasing involves partnering with your psyche on many levels and allowing yourself to feel those uncomfortable, pent-up emotions, reframing your role in the events. But you're not just releasing the sting of what happened. Remember those ego states surrounding the raw spot you learned about in Chapter 3? Now you're invited to heal or release parts that your subconscious created to protect you from that raw spot and from the pain it held for you. Like my identity around not being worthy of love, which protected me as a child from the hurt of being rejected. When I no longer wear the mask of unlovable, my vantage point is empowered, and I can better release the pain.

Sometimes, my clients balk at this step. Let's face it: we probably walk into a therapist's office expecting to heal the raw spots we'll uncover and put an end to our suffering. Ideally, we hope to achieve this by quickly talking about our pain, focusing on the positive things in our lives, and hanging our hopes on a brighter future. I get it. At first glance, this step seems kind of fruitless, expending precious energy and time focusing on pain.

Who wants to sign up for that? Then, as my clients begin identifying their raw spots, they're more willing to do the inner work because they keep feeling better the further they go.

Holding and releasing unlocks the power of your mind, where you can access free will and break free from attachment imprints calling the shots in your life. In this chapter, you'll read about rebounding after trust is broken and how to encourage yourself to drop the defenses around vulnerable raw spots. I share Part I of a two-part story of a time I was blindsided by betrayal and the therapeutic process that helped me regain my sense of self. Then you'll learn the tools of holding and releasing, plus their function in the brain-body connection. Once you arrive at the gap where free will resides, you won't want to ever go back.

FROM EXCRUCIATING PAIN TO EMPOWERMENT

Trust injuries in our most intimate relationships are the type of events that force people to seek refuge, grounding, healing, and clarity. One such example is betrayal by a loved one. Today, trust is on my mind because I'm heading into the office this morning to meet with a client who, after thirty years of marriage to the love of his life, found out that she had betrayed him. By this client's admission in a previous session, he never would've sought healing for the utterly excruciating pain in his heart. But he entered therapy recently exhausted from having attempted every tool to ease the pain, and he was out of moves to pull himself out of complete despair.

Now, he's open to *entertaining* an option he didn't previously consider: to enter a more profound level of understanding that brings him up close and personal with the vulnerable part of himself that believes "I am inadequate in connecting in relationships." That's the lie about himself that he must release to continue with the step of integration that I teach in Chapter 5. He's been learning why this false belief about himself feels so ingrained. It's tied to parts of his identity he's held since childhood, like an overachiever, a sarcastic wise guy, and the part he calls "lazy" that continuously pulls him into a place of passivity and not pursuing his wife. All these ego states come with good intentions to prevent him from the risk of "rejection." But as we have learned, this self-preservation comes at a cost. Vital raw spots we need to heal get pushed into our subconscious, where they fester.

With precision in the therapeutic process, we're clear on where we systematically need to go, and miracles can happen quickly. After just a few short hours of therapy, this client began to connect his ego states with raw spots from his youth. He felt socially inadequate as a child and felt not trying was his best option to avoid being pushed away. As he accessed parts of himself hidden in his subconscious and examined them in the light, he perceived his inner child's agenda in perpetuating his "inadequate to connect" NC. They were trying to keep him safe by not trying to connect so he couldn't be hurt if his wife bailed on him. So, those parts were a big source of why he wasn't making meaningful connections in his relationships, which was hurting him.

Just imagine how this wisdom can be a power tool for improving his connections with others, no matter what happens with his marriage. He can become proactive and vulnerable in relationships. If he's that version of himself, she could still cheat, but he'll be less likely to blame himself and instead put his energy toward discernment, which you'll read about later in this book.

ARMED RESISTANCE

Holding requires more than reflecting on the past and chanting "Omm." Your subconscious works overtime—with the fervor that Frodo protects the shire, his homeland, in *Lord of the Rings*—to protect you from the raw spots beyond your awareness. In personality development, where the child's paramount goal is to stay connected to the attachment figure at all costs, we can appreciate what's at stake for the child when the bond between child and parent is threatened. We learn to bury our vulnerable raw spots and keep them hidden to protect that bond. Our ego states come online and form the personality structure, obscuring the tender place. For example, a child sensing that they can't share their sadness because they don't feel worthy in the eyes of mom and dad may push that vulnerability underground. They might instead take on a performance-driven, jokester spirit that never removes their "fix-it hat." These personas or ego states help the child survive without showing their insecurity around worthiness by preventing them from wondering why they feel so emotionally disconnected from themselves and others.

Wearing the armor of our personality comes at a cost. John. C. Pierrakos describes the armored man as internally divided–the mind from the body, the body from the emotions, and the emotions from the spirit. This sets an individual up to live what Pierrakos calls an "antilife," in which they're so internally disconnected, they can't connect with others on the outside.

But. . . wouldn't feeling the sadness lead to depression? Feeling our painful emotions along a pathway to joy seems paradoxical—on the surface. A client brought this up just last week as we discussed how he doesn't want to "hold" his sadness. I invited him to access his feeling of inadequacy, and he explicitly refused.

Client: I'm not going there. That's what everyone in my family does, and that's why they're all depressed!

Me: Do you know what depression actually is?

Client: No.

Me: It's not a result of feeling sad. Depression is a result of an inability to feel sadness.

That's right. Silencing one emotion (in his case, sadness) has a way of depressing the entire system.

Our armored guard parts (or the *"honchos,"* as renowned psychotherapist and author Sandra Paulsen refers to them; Richard Shwartz calls them "protector parts") have agendas to keep us safe, believing that "if

I own the fullness of my emotions, I'll lose connection with my attachment figure, and I may die without them." So, they resist allowing the adult self to hold the sadness, thus keeping the vulnerable part safe from feeling exposed and alone.

You may feel already well-acquainted with the raw spot's pain. It has often chafed you for years, and you may be ready to dive into your ego states like an Olympic swimmer. For others, this may be the first time you've considered a particular raw spot, and it might feel as shocking as the moment in *Star Wars* when Luke and Darth Vader are battling it out with lightsabers; then he drops the bombshell, "Luke. . . I am your father."

Resurrecting buried, vulnerable emotions threatens the subconscious's defense system, sending our ego states into kicking and screaming to "back off!" If these guards had a voice, they might say something such as, "Why should I let you in now to help this sad/lonely/terrified child when doing so will just leave him disconnected from those he loves and just sitting alone in his pain?" Again, good intentions. Remember, we imprint these scripts at an early age and hold decades of energy and build stories that reinforce the system of NCs we believe.

Untangling this knot requires care. Like anything stuck in place for many years, these parts of ourselves aren't eager to loosen their grip. They often cling tighter to the narrative when the walls they guard are questioned. In therapy, a significant amount of time and patience is imperative for the therapist and client to address the guards' objections. We must strategically recognize and release emotional and cognitive blocks that keep us from connecting with hidden, vital parts of the self in the subconscious. Note: Resistant ego states don't tend to soften if we enter into a battle with them. Instead, we may find ourselves at a deadlock. Instead, when guards continue to appear, we work with the allowance we have.

Engaging the armored ego states first requires us to extend them a massive dose of appreciation for their efforts to keep us safe. When we gain their trust, we may enlist their help in a new mission to allow us into the more tender areas. There, we discover our inner child who experienced the raw spot and believes a distorted view of self-blame.

Whether you've tried to heal a particular spot before or not, the challenge is to proceed without avoiding or disassociating from a raw spot's emotional pain, especially since we're in a lot of pain about how we feel someone did us wrong. "Dissociation" is a psychology term for the disconnect between our conscious selves from parts of us buried in our subconsciousness (for survival, as stated in Chapter 1's "The Root of Taking Things Personally" section). Holding requires reconnection between the two, which isn't as easy as putting a cell phone on a charger. For starters, you go inward to find the lost cell phone. And check the messages.

Holding what needs to be released requires intentionality, preciseness, compassion, and a road map to find what's lost. Signposts on the road to these hidden parts of our selves are everywhere when you know what to look for, such as those repetitive patterns in your life that continually confront you with unrelenting pain, confusion, and disillusionment. Along the way, look for any unmet needs of your inner child that need to be met. Perhaps there's a part that needed an offer of emotional presence by an attachment figure and never received it. Or a part that still longs to be told they are okay just as they are and that performing in overdrive all the time isn't necessary to keep relationships intact. Another longing many of us carry is the need to feel that it is safe to have a voice and be able to express it. As we tend to our unmet needs, the ego states put down their armor. No need for resistance.

MY JOURNEY PART I

A few years ago, a series of life events brought on an avalanche of NCs, and I was swept under and engulfed by boundless misery. Betrayed by a colleague with whom I thought I was in a harmonious work environment, then in a flash, they and another officemate ambushed me with an eviction notice. Effective immediately.

That happened on a Friday, and I had nowhere to see my clients the coming Monday. On the drive home, tears streamed down my face; I was hyperventilating—barely able to see the road before me. A heart-wrenching blow had flattened me on every level—heart, mind, body, and spirit. I thought these things only happened in the movies. And yet there I was in the midst of drama with no camera in sight.

What just happened? What could I have done to deserve that sort of treatment? It must be me. Those thoughts relentlessly looped in my mind. I mean, just a week prior, the officemate who led the pack had reached out to ask how my ski trip was. Feeling starkly rejected by officemates, I couldn't entertain any other narrative surrounding my view of self. Not to mention. . . *How could I have missed the signs that they felt this way about me? Did I have some terrible blind spot that kept me from seeing danger signs in the form of character flaws in others? —Signs that pointed to parts of others that were less than ideal?* I recognized how my self-blaming voices were trying to shield me. . . *from what raw spot?*

Searching to answer that question, I forced myself into my therapist's office. My ego state imprinted with the negative cognition, "I am not lovable," was up in arms. The betrayal, when I had been nothing but accommodating, had forced the bottom to drop out of my very sense of self.

My therapist and I excavated my raw spots with an intensity I never knew existed. I peeled myself away from the seductive, self-deprecating spiral in which we're the victim and the other the perpetrator. You know, the stories that, long after the narrative is well-worn, we hold onto like our favorite comfy blanket—although it's now wet and moldy. Well, the mildew finally got to me. Simply revisiting the origin of my pain wasn't going to cut it. I decided to open space and go further to access and connect with a younger part of me, permitting her to share more of her story. We connected with a part of me I thought was mostly healed: I am unlovable.

The adult me served as the witness to this inner child's story. Witnessing is far from a passive role. In fact, the Old English root of "witness" is *witnes*, which means to have knowledge and understanding of something. So, when we enter the story of the inner child, we seek to hold their experience with all its pieces, including emotions. This is the path to allowing the vulnerable parts of the self to feel deeply seen and held in their pain or fear (something they were unable to do at the time the original wound was inflicted). Through witnessing our inner child, we create the conditions for what the Buddha calls "ultimate healing," accessed through self-compassion.

For the sake of brevity, I invite you into a shortened version of my experience of connecting with my inner child, knowing there are many more steps therapists employ to get to the furthest abyss of oneself. Conjuring an image of ourselves at the earliest age we recall the feeling can help us bring an inner child and their story to life. In my case, "I am not lovable," took me back to the age of six. Specifically, it was a school picture, me in pigtails, with a somewhat flattened facial expression. Decades spent living life kept me from ever stopping to get curious about her experience at that age. And now, here I was slowing down long enough, for the first time in my life, to notice the look on her face in that picture was a complete juxtaposition from how I (and others) would've described me – funny, energetic, life of the party, or jovial. I was intrigued, curious, and open.

With the therapist's guidance, I invited my inner child to sit on my lap and share why she felt unloved (a more detailed process is outlined in the back of the chapter). This part of myself shared her entire experience surrounding why she felt so unlovable from a place of presence and vulnerability. I asked her questions; she answered. I validated; she heard. I extended compassion; she received it. I continued to open space for more sharing; she had more to say to fill up that space. I comforted; she received. I began to see and know; she felt seen and known. This dance of giving and receiving formed a connection between us in the core of my being. I took on a more grounded presence. A presence through which my interaction with self, others, and all the universe began to feel more meaningful. (I'll unpack this in the next chapter).

The events with my officemates reminded me how self-enlightenment isn't always linear. Just when we think we have reached a point of self-actualization that would afford us a buffer from future pain in and from human relationships, the universe offers us more grist for the mill. In this fashion, the universe always has our back.

HOLD AND RELEASE

Holding and releasing is a big ask when we want a quick fix that propels us directly into the land of nirvana. Except that, as Carl Jung, one of the psychotherapy greats of all time, teaches: we achieve nirvana, or as he would say, transcendence, by shedding our "false selves," which blame us for things we had no control over. As we slough off the false selves, layer upon layer, a more nuanced, truer, and whole self is revealed. This is an ongoing process, so expect to be in a state of "completing." As long as we practice these tools, we may continue shedding layers of the false self throughout our lives.

Floating back. . .

Accessing the most vulnerable parts of our being can sometimes require the patience of a saint, as the inner child may not trust the adult to meet needs. However, the payoff is incredible. With a carefully formed alliance between adult and child, we begin to release the false identities (such as "I'm not loveable") we have clung to for decades.

The ultimate healing conditions are possible when the adult is well-resourced and demonstrates the bandwidth to metabolize the child's experience. (assuming the adult self has been shored up in the process). For example, maybe the adult can show the inner child how their adult self is safe and cared for and all of their areas of competence, how they shine and are trusted by friends, family members, and colleagues. Then, most importantly and powerfully, is the patience to stay tuned into the child and validate their every feeling and move. . . *A very mature adult thing to do* (validating and extending compassion).

Consider the following scene. . . As the adult, you sit on a bench near a playground. A child close by falls and, as children do, runs to you wailing in complete desperation in utter panic for comfort. Most adults know how to rush in immediately and tend to this situation. They use their steady presence to calm the child down and assure the child that the adult will take care of all the child's needs. The adult's presence and the energy in their words bring comfort and peace to the child as they trust the adult to heal their wound.

Now consider that same adult can't tend to the child

because they were not tended to in that way by their attachment figures, leaving the child feeling suspended with unmet needs. Or the adult makes the child's pain about themselves. So, the child loses trust in the adult's ability to provide care. This lack of trust from child to adult shows up in our inner worlds as well. This nuanced work requires that the adult meet their inner child and demonstrate a different experience that allows the inner child to grow trust in the adult. Sometimes, the child can't make eye contact with the adult, as if to say, I haven't been able to depend on you until now to take care of my needs; why should I trust you now?

The adult may have an impoverished view of self, as in overly identifying with the insecure ego states driving the bus. Then, the adult can be flooded with powerful emotions we may resist or defend against, abandoning our child in the process. For this reason, we need a therapist present to support us and redirect the conversation in a therapeutic way. Time must be dedicated to bringing adaptive information to the adult so they can meet the inner child's needs. This leads the adult observer to develop the emotional tolerance to hold the inner child's experience.

Sometimes clients who've come to terms with their parents or other attachment figures over the years (claiming, for example, that "they" did the best they could, and I have forgiven them) are reluctant to give the inner child a microphone, lest they air grievances we believed to be long resolved. But I didn't mention blaming anyone (including parents or other attachment figures). The inner child presents their testimony, which can be powerfully healing even after the adult has moved on from what happened.

The therapist will coach us to connect with our vulnerable parts by orienting the client to observe the inner child (vulnerable part) from the place of observer, or what the Buddha calls the mindful one—the place from which we can see all other parts of the personality system. That vantage point is within our being before picking up any ego states with their distorted messages. We can step into the observer role because, as David Epstein explains in *The 12 Stages of Healing*, our adult self ". . . know[s] that we are separate from our distress, or the source of our suffering." As witnesses, we can identify with the inner child's experience of having suffered, "without 'taking it personally.'"

I lead my clients to imagine engaging their inner child; together, they take an incredible time machine or magic carpet ride. The destinations are past scenes that once held triggers, such as when their dad spoke in a harsh tone that landed on the child's sensitive, developing view of self, causing an imprint of "I'm not enough." Other examples may include when the child felt neglected by mom because she was too busy with her activities, or when they were bullied in the 8th grade (I was) after having just moved to a new school. That time in my life only solidified my already impoverished view of self and reinforced my feelings of profound loneliness.

As we allow the movie of our life story to roll, we trust the wisdom of the process as we open space for whatever bubbles up, knowing that it is beckoning to be healed (rewritten). There is a melting away of what we once felt to be true about who we were, the false selves. Organically, a new view of self begins to emerge. Scene by scene, the well-resourced adult self enters the story with the child in tow. They write a new script, allowing the child (felt sense in the body) to relive the scene the way it could have/should have been. Thus, the adult takes their feelings out of the mercy of others' actions or inactions years ago, shifting the narrative to one of greater agency and self-determination. Think of this process as the adult creating and downloading new cognitions (I am enough) through the new lens (gathered by the work from chapters 1-3). This leads to a more whole view of self.

For example, a woman overcoming eating disorders brought her adult-level resources and experience to memories of shame around her body. She had always felt she had no right to take up space. Then, she revisited her inner child in experiences where she learned that false self and saturated her child with the new feeling of "I deserve to be my true self," regardless of what others may have said or done.

These scenes of release provide fertile ground for rewiring our view of self and all its parts. For example, her perfectionist ego state can accept a new role, such as healthy body image advocate, as she rewrites the new script and narrative of who she is and what she believes about herself. And since the brain isn't aware of the difference between what is real or perceived and has no concept of time, she experiences a new, present event as she connects with her inner child. This process allows the nervous system to calm down as new, adaptive information and safe responses to external events reinforce the new view of self. The next time something happens that would make her start hating her body, she will have new receptors to more easily access healthy adaptive information that will allow her to choose to love it instead.

Looking forward...

Having floated to the past and created more of an embodied sense of "I deserve to be my true self," she's now even more confident in handling her relationships and social engagements with more ease and a sense of agency. These changes are subtle but profound and powerful; instead of spending social time comparing her body and counting calories, she can connect with those around her. At the subconscious level, which dictates behavior, her new scripts are so fully integrated that she's not remotely reminded of those discarded, old obsessions.

The holding and releasing process allows us to shift into a truer self. Now that we have access to those once disconnected parts of ourselves, we have the rich opportunity to continue exploring the message until it is fully felt, embodied on a profound level, and we begin to naturally feel a felt sense of "I am lovable" or "I am enough."

Through integration, which is the topic of Chapter 5, we start to see the world through our new eyes versus seeing ourselves through others' eyes. The client recovering from an eating disorder no longer cares what others think of her body (or what she thinks they think), and I no longer care if others think I'm lovable or not. This shift translates into moving through our worlds in new ways without self-judgment or taking on perceived negativity from others. Homeostasis, or inner harmony, becomes our new norm as heart and mind are congruent and not easily thrown off by external factors. We feel more confident in embodying our new self-cognitions, presenting our new, empowered selves to the world.

BRAIN-BODY CONNECTION

Neuroscience has caught up to ancient philosophy, showing us how we transform our brain's patterns as we shift the inner child's narrative from one of victimhood to a sense of agency, where they are grounded with more feelings of authority over their place in the world, including moving up from a place of powerlessness, and into a place of control. That new reality becomes an embodied, felt sense—their powerfulness feels as true as their lack of power had felt before.

Know who your inner child has been confiding in all these years and who has their back no matter what? Your body. When a raw spot originates, the nervous system is often dysregulated, caught in a flight, flee, or freeze mode. Due to our false self's messages frozen in time, our sensitive nervous systems may stay hypervigilant to contain pent-up emotions. This impacts our view of self and others, setting us up to perceive threats where none exist. So, as you hold and release, your body needs to participate in the process. When doing emotionally healing work, we can't leave the somatic piece at the door. In fact, it must be central to healing any injuries on the nervous system.

It was once believed that once our brains were

developed, everything was locked in place. However, the science of neuroplasticity has proven that throughout our lives we can create new pathways. This possibility can be exciting for us, whether we are trying to learn a new instrument or a new language or trying to change our view of self and others, hence changing our experience in the world, including our dynamics with others.

Neuropathways holding new information are created, and the inner child gives over the old script they were holding and transforms the story into a healthier, better-informed view of self and others. It is inevitable that even after we've done all this holding and releasing, others will trigger our raw spots. The nervous system may have been soothed through all the previous inner work, but we're still in the body, and our humanness is still limited by the body. We can expect that little triggers will continue to present themselves and provide signposts that lead us into new depths of discovery, growth. Integration. Our frontal lobe cortex is always accessible; we have the tools to calm a dysregulated nervous system and bring it into balance. This part of the brain is responsible for wisdom, reason, and logic; it can bring awareness to and connect with parts of our identities (ego states) that hold the distorted views of self lodged and encoded in the nervous system.

WHERE FREE WILL RESIDES

"Between stimulus and response there is a space. In that space is our power to choose response. In our response lies our growth and freedom."

—VIKTOR FRANKL

If you don't choose the road in life, the road gets chosen for you. The previous steps of growing in awareness of our original wound, how we identify the raw spot, and then holding and releasing the false self (NCs) allows our nervous system to move out of constriction/fight or flight mode. Our nervous system becomes regulated and able to tend to reality, versus being hyperstimulated by the illusions that we once bought into. This can translate to how we react to our neighbors getting together for a dinner party and not inviting us; instead of responding with anger, believing "I'm not enough," we have space to take a breath. We can remember that it's not personal and CHOOSE to reject the NC for a belief that warrants a neutral—or even positive—response. This lays the groundwork in the nervous system to create our free will. Oh, wait, aren't we supposed to have free will already?

Most people believe we have some sense of agency over our lives and that we choose our paths. However, we may not have as much control as we think. Since the 1980s, neuroscientists such as Benjamin Libet and, more recently, John Dylan Haynes, have found that our brain knows between four to ten seconds in advance what we will do before the self decides and takes action.

Biometry researcher Hans Liljenström, finds that faster decisions are based on emotion and memory, whereas slower decisions allow for more "cognitive deliberation," or rational choice. If feelings and prior experience dictate much of our actions, how much free will could we actually have? Given these numbers, we're practically running on autopilot! Upon investigating our inner worlds and how they manifest in our choices, we may realize how much of our paths are dictated by our original/inner programming. We might have much freedom over our life choices and those we continue to make than we thought.

The majority of our so-called "decisions" aren't so much ours (as our modern-day world would have us believe) as the response to the tracks of our neuropathways. *Essentially, our brains are wired not to have free will.* Not convinced? Think of a recent trigger that held some emotional charge. Notice your response. How much agency did you have in your reaction? How wide was the gap between trigger and reaction? If we don't choose to widen the gap between sting and reactivity, we likely remain at the mercy of the burdened parts buried in the unconscious. Therefore, the road gets chosen for us. We give our power away. The NPP illuminates the option to reconsider free will and disentangle it from our distorted view of self.

We may choose our path anew as we step into a clearer view of self. We might tap into the few seconds between decision and action, where original ideas are born, and we have a sense of freedom, wonder, and curiosity. Our sense of agency/control and self-determination reside here. So, why not step into a greater reality and make decisions from a place of free thinking? The key is to widen the gap where rational choice resides; I'm referring to creating space between trigger and reaction. Here, we find true power and control—that is, what we actually have control over.

Holding and releasing allows us to reclaim power over our lives from the external forces that have governed many of our experiences. Growing awareness of the roots of taking things personally clears some space in the psyche to entertain ideas of another path. There, we can glimpse the choice between feeling the sting of hurt and the automatic reactivity that tends to follow. In this gap lies free will. I continue unpacking this notion in the coming chapters as we explore how to widen the space between trigger and our response. This is the seat of free will and power.

Through integration, which I cover in the next chapter, the gap between trigger and action becomes very bridgeable. We form new neuropathways that connect unknown parts of the self with our higher-functioning prefrontal cortex—and all its wisdom, logic, and reason. Then we can soar to new heights, from which we may reflect upon the same upsetting experiences in a fresh way. Our new perspectives pave the way for us to become changed people who know it's never personal.

POINTS OF CONTEMPLATION

Through holding and releasing, the mind is better-resourced to react more thoughtfully and deliberately when a raw spot is triggered. Complete the following questions to begin widening the gap between trigger and reaction.

- Consider a raw spot you identified in your Chapter 3 Contemplation. Conjure a resistant feeling connected to the emotion you would rather not process. What is the resistance about? What might you be afraid will happen?

- Notice where you feel the resistance to a hurt—sadness, loneliness, betrayal—in your body. Close your eyes and place a hand on that discomfort. Send it a message like, "It's nice to finally connect with you in this new way." Then describe any somatic or emotional shifts you experience.

- Imagine a peace come over you as you feel more connected to this place where free will, creativity, and a feeling of congruency reside. Remember a recent event when you reacted more quickly than you wished. Now revisit that scene in the moment between the trigger and your reaction. Pause the action here. What information do you see that you may have missed before? How else might you have responded?

CHAPTER 5

Integrating the Whole: View of Self

"People are not disturbed by things, but by the view they take of them."

—EPICTETUS

Why do I think that I'm the exception to the rule? On the day of the tennis match, I expect to win—and do it by showing up to one hour-long lesson a week to work on my swing pattern, fine-tune my serve, tweak my grip, rehearse strategy, and then carry on throughout the week with my usual schedule. This nearly universal desire for a quick, easy path follows well-trodden neuropathways that span decades; our amygdala wires the brain to avoid pain (tiger) and seek pleasure (safety and comfort). Changing our course in life may feel virtually impossible! If you've ever been driving down an unpaved country road and tried to veer off, you'll appreciate how quickly your car is pulled back into the well-worn ruts on the road. Rewiring neuropathways requires time, patience, and precise attention to direct our thoughts toward a new path.

During a recent conversation with a tennis pro, I was reminded that what makes tennis players great is the time dedicated between the lessons to sharpen their skills. This translates into a winning advantage on the court. The same holds true for many areas of life, including the steps to let things go that we've taken personally. I often tell my clients that while powerful, one hour in a therapy session isn't usually sufficient to translate into real, lasting change. Transformation happens between sessions as the client practices widening the gap between trigger and response to make new choices and create new experiences for themselves.

We transcend our hurt feelings by integrating the truth beneath the false beliefs and attending to our unmet needs. Through individuation, which is the focus of this chapter, we emerge as more authentic versions of ourselves, and we can move on from past hurts. *Finally.* In this chapter, you'll read Part II of my story, in which I hold and release tender pieces of my story, bringing new info to my younger, vulnerable self. You'll also learn how we can connect with the deepest parts of our being, even our ancestors and our shadows. Energy we were expending to erect and reinforce walls of protection (keeping others out and us locked in dysfunctional patterns) is now freed up and can be directed toward being curious, open to adaptive information, and accessible to self.

INTEGRATION/INDIVIDUATION

During integration, the inner/wounded child gets to speak their experience, releasing their pain to the adult who holds the space to embrace the fullness of the story. We give the inner child the voice they didn't get to express at the time of the wounding. They're witnessed by a compassionate, present, attentive, interested, wise, constant companion—our adult self. When our adult-self shows up for our inner child this way, both parts fully integrate into the whole self. This illuminates the power and beauty in this vulnerable part, which is finally receiving something they never had before.

There's practically no limit to the possibilities with this tool/exercise of integration, called "Future Template" in the EMDR space. In session, I invite the client to conjure up an image that represents a situation or encounter in which they would like to see some shifts in perspective, to download some of their new positive cognitions. The client imagines playing out the new way they will feel and react and what they will say when their raw spot might be triggered. We also consider multiple potential responses they could receive and how no matter what, the client will remain grounded, confident, and hold their inner child. This way, we can share with a partner, "I feel lonely," without the expectation that they will save us from feeling sad; instead, we seek to be deeply seen, known, and held by them. Regardless of their response, when we enter relationships offering our fullness (without burdening the other with our NCs for them to fix), we lay the foundation for a safe, supportive connection.

No issue is off the table in the Future Template exercise, and over the years, I've seen powerful transformations take place before my very eyes. The businessman who suffers from the imposter syndrome and wants to further embody his new view of self when he is speaking at the upcoming board meeting. The client who feels panicked at the idea of spending time with the family during the upcoming holidays, lest she be pulled back into old triggers and dysfunctional dynamics with mom and dad. The husband who, for years, has kept silent in moments of upset in the marriage, feeling powerless at not having a voice, is now shored up by new connections with his vulnerable (inner child) part. He continues integrating the new positive cognition: "It is safe to have a voice, and I deserve to speak my needs." Basking in this new feeling, he honors himself more.

The integration process dissolves our greatest attachment frame fears—annihilation if we were rejected or abandoned. As we merge with our vulnerable part/pain and let go of beliefs we thought kept us safe, we now come to see those scripts were all an illusion. With a rewired nervous system, we can experience an event that would've triggered our defenses in the past. Still, now that we're an integrated "whole self" with the adult and inner child together, we emerge a more powerful, resilient human. This allows us to grow in tolerating some of the heaviness of emotions we couldn't handle before.

Where we once had ego states that quickly barred our connection with our delicate emotions, now we have a greater bandwidth to be with those feelings. Much-needed emotional presence is opened within the self. Perhaps such that we're no longer triggered by things we used to take personally. We feel safe no matter what happens externally. Well. . . at least more than before.

We're "integrating," not "integrated." In its infinite wisdom, the universe will continue to provide opportunities for us to grow into the fullest versions of ourselves no matter how much inner work we do. All roads—or triggers—lead back to our wounded parts and our view of self. Any resistance or blocks point toward a need to first look within. That always needs to be where the / journey/trail begins. As I often say to clients, we need to make a U-Turn and look under our own hood first.

The further we integrate, the more confident we grow that we can bend and change, becoming more whole versions of ourselves. No longer clinging so tightly to egos, we're freed up to move with the energy that pulsates throughout the entire universe. There is more congruence in the heart, mind, and body, which translates into feelings of peace, calm, and connectedness versus constriction.

MY JOURNEY PART II

In the last chapter, I shared My Journey Part I, describing a heartbreaking event of my officemates suddenly evicting me from our office and my therapeutic process to heal from that experience. Finally, after holding my inner child's pain and longing to be accepted and releasing it, I came to a calm, neutral realization: *What if my colleagues' actions toward me weren't about me—but about them?* Not what I could've done or not done, but perhaps they'd revealed their own insecurities and damaged inner worlds. We don't always get to glimpse into their story, but in this instance, I did. As time passed, I learned one of them was fired from an institution I was associated with, as well as left a trail of carnage in her wake, reflected by the people's hearts she seriously damaged. Another officemate was notoriously challenging to work with and was removed from her previous office (hence her eagerness to get me to sign a lease with her).

For them to have treated me more kindly, they would've had to walk through their own fires and grow into healthier versions of themselves. (Versions that would set them up to have healthier relationships with themselves and others). This type of insight is invaluable to share with the inner child. Mine needed to hear that she *was* loveable, but those people weren't equipped to love her—and that was on them. Our adult may share more general messages, too, such as, "You did not deserve that treatment back then." This compassion allows the child to feel profoundly validated, safe, and held. With this safety, they can let go of the false self and begin to see themselves more truly and with self-compassion. Our adult self may now integrate with this inner child, forming a more complete version of the whole self.

GENERATIONAL CLEARING

Any work that encircles the journey of releasing false views of self would be deficient without incorporating the much-needed and often overlooked work of clearing out patterns that glom onto us from emotional and psychological burdens that get passed down to us from generational and cultural traumas. I have worked with countless individuals who, after having done thorough trauma work with their parts in explicit memories, find that something still feels stuck "on a cellular level." This stuckness resides less in details of specific memory than in an implicit memory that may have encoded before you acquired language—even in the womb—and beyond your lived experience. Therefore, your mind has no way to access this friction point. Neither can traditional modalities like talk therapy. The totality of the self, once thought to be your story and all its contents contained by your sole experience in your mind and body, is now being proven to expand beyond explicit memory and it a new frontier of implicit memory.

Fortunately, if we learned our fear responses from our families of origin, often spanning generations, there are tools specifically for releasing our inherited scripts. Modern science's quest to reach into the *great unknown* of the psyche has launched countless professionals in the fields of biology and psychology (and the quantum field) to study *epigenetics*. This field investigates how we inherit traits and traumas of previous generations through gene transcription. Their findings provide methods for further integration of the energy tied up in our ego states; this occurs through transmissions from one generation to the next on a cellular *and* a metaphysical level. In the 1960s, our dual inheritances were coined by philosopher Eugene T. Gendlin as the "felt sense." Think of the felt sense as a bodily, visceral reaction that doesn't reflect our experiences or views, such as an inexplicable fear of heights or a knee-jerk response to being cut off in traffic.

Parts of the self that have seemed mysterious begin making sense through studying epigenetics. You learned in Chapter 1 of this book that our imprints are forming in the womb. Dr. Peter W. Nathanielsz writes about this epigenetic plasticity in *In Life in the Womb*, saying: "There is mounting evidence that programming of lifetime health by the conditions in the womb is equally, if not more important, than our genes in determining how we perform mentally and physically during life." Scripts we learned in utero help us make meaning of our experiences through felt sense. To heal our raw spots in the body's felt senses, we must explore them and find what needs to be released.

In searching our felt senses, we find that our ancestors' past traumas are imprinted into the fabric of our being—our cells—through genetic mutations. This is traced back to the organic matter that became our eggs when our mothers were in utero, or the "germ line." Professor of psychiatry and neuroscientist Rachel Yehuda has found PTSD and high stress-related gene modifications in parents, which affected the children's stress responses. Yehuda writes in *The Scientific American* that we don't know if those altered genes ". . . are necessarily markers of vulnerability or whether they may reflect a mechanism through which offspring become better equipped to cope with diversity." Author Mark Wolynn describes this as "secondary PTSD" in his book, *It Didn't Start With You.* He has developed tools for somatic integration of raw spots held in our felt senses.

Whether the PTSD adaptations increase resilience

or not, there's ample research that our environment and experiences continue shaping our genetics throughout life, so we can reprogram old scripts that don't work for us—even those we were born with. Wolynn is one of several leaders in the psychology lane of epigenetics, along with Sandra Paulsen, author of *When There Are No Words*. They're helping practitioners navigate the complex inner worlds of their clients and assist clients in discovering new depths within themselves.

The imprints from our experiences and those we inherited may look strikingly similar at first glance. Here's a list of a few common signs of generational trauma:

- Feelings of hopelessness with no clear reason why we would feel this way

- Abusive behaviors: mental, physical, and substance abuse that can clearly be connected to prior generations

- A poverty mindset that grips individuals and leaves them feeling powerless to develop a healthy relationship with money and their worthiness of prosperity

- Fears of rejection that are not able to be traced back to any explicit memory

- Lack of confidence that is clearly seen throughout previous generations

- Intense feelings of loneliness, and we can't recall a time of not feeling this way (cellular level)

If you deal with some of the above issues, consider

that maybe those feelings don't always stem from a story in your lifetime—so things that feel personal, perhaps aren't personal to you. At all. They may have been passed down to you—uninvited. Generational NCs can affect descendants of Holocaust survivors, enslaved people, and too many other historical atrocities to name, not to mention intrapersonal and interpersonal themes that have plagued humans since the dawn of civilization.

Generational healing is a process known by many names: "ancestral unburdening" to the IFS camp, "breaking generational curses" in Christian circles, and commonly "healing family wounds" in psychology. When exploring this work, don't overlook some not-so-obvious areas of exploration that impact our psyche and view of self in the world. Perhaps we can call these the Under-The-Radar Impacts, such as Loss of culture, Climate change, Genocide, Extinction of Species, Terrorism, Self-Disgust, Forsaken Qualities, and Alienation. We identify these raw spots with a fundamental principle of generational clearing: Our deceased family members want us to release, but first, we need to be aware of their pain. By becoming aware of our ancestors' pain, we can help them unburden it. This process mirrors much of the first three steps of the NPP.

The ritual at the last stop on the generational healing journey is breathtaking. Every time I have the honor to lead a client through this deep work, they receive a sacred gift from their ancestor—often an apology or clarity around what happened. Clearing generational trauma can be a two-way street. They have support to offer us, too. I always remind clients that our deceased ancestors have never been so much in their pure state than where they are now, on the other side. So, they hold the treasures and impart the greatest of all great wisdom on us. We simply need to listen. Call these epigenetics methods what you will. I don't doubt that experiences from past generations impact our daily experiences. You may, too, as you explore this new field.

INTEGRATING THROUGH SHADOW WORK

People often look at me like I've got lobsters coming out of my ears when I tell them that one of the quickest ways to access and integrate the disowned parts of ourselves is to *love what we dislike in others* Notice I wrote "quick," as in "simple," but certainly not easy. Yet, I would be remiss in sharing ways we integrate the self without offering this as an effective and powerful tool. The personality traits, behaviors, and attitudes we dislike (and find attractive) in others are projections of our hidden selves. In Jeremiah Abrams and Connie Zweig's book, Meeting the Shadow, they observe that "We see the shadow mostly indirectly, in the distasteful traits and actions of other people, out there where it is safer to observe it, since we cannot look directly into this hidden domain." There resides our shadow self, the disowned parts of our personalities that were too threatening to portray when we were younger, since having them may have meant a severing with our attachment figures.

Some of our personality characteristics were celebrated by parents, teachers, and society in general, shaping our identity. Hence, we keep those traits center stage.

Other aspects of ourselves were considered unacceptable and immoral–laziness, anger, and stinginess—or undesirable—loudness, needing help, and failure. Abrams and Zweig quote Jungian analyst, Marie Louise von Franz, saying:

> The shadow plunges man into the immediacy of situations here and now, and thus creates the real biography of the human being, who is always inclined to assume he is only what he thinks he is. It is the biography created that shadow that counts.

The parts of our shadow self are buried beyond the periphery of our awareness. Abrams and Zweig say the shadow is ". . . dangerous, disorderly, and forever in hiding, as if the light of consciousness would steal its very life." However, integrating these ego states can yield profound relief to the psyche.

Shadow work is a rich and expansive body of psychology that dissects the inner workings of our unconscious in a way that helps make sense of our perceptions of others and self, as well as offers an approach to healing the parts that keep us stuck with parts that cause suffering to ourselves and those around us. Essentially, all roads lead back to the self. So, do we have the courage (or guts) to allow for curiosity of those often-subtle nudges that life presents us with in the form of triggers from our encounters with others?

Sure, we think and believe that "it" is happening to us and that irritating traits in others are their baggage they need to work out on their journey to enlightenment. But as we evolve in our thinking, we realize true power resides in embracing that "we see the world as we are." Settling into that truth, we access a teaching from *A Course in Miracles* that states, *We give everything we see the meaning it has to us.* This is to say, the egoic parts of our mind assign meaning and narratives to everything, every being, and every situation. So, we can reassign the meaning of something we took personally (or found the trait in the other irritating) and revise our narrative. We can change our heart and mind to believe what the other person may've said or done means nothing, something benign, or even something positive.

For example, recently, I went to the neighborhood grocery store just after walking my dog, so I was in gym clothes with no makeup, hoping not to run into anyone I know. In the produce section, I spotted a colleague who lives nearby, whom I was planning to reach out to about putting flyers for my upcoming workshop in his office. He's very tall and gregarious, a larger-than-life kind of person. He greeted me warmly, and I didn't want to hug him because I was sweaty, but he insisted. We caught up with each other, and he came to my car with me to get the flyers.

As I drove away, I noticed that I was running a script of both warm feelings for having shared a few pleasantries with him, along with a low-grade, slightest bit of somatic disturbance. *Hmmm, what was the latter one about?* The warm feelings came from the surprise of running into a dear friend at the store, him mentioning "getting lunch on the calendar soon," and his acknowledgement and apology for not having time to read the first couple chapters of my book (which by the way, he eagerly and excitingly agreed to do several months prior over lunch). Mixed in with the yumminess and warmth of the genuine and mutual admiration we have for each other is a similar sense of humor that runs at the same frequency.

So, what was this somatic disturbance I felt in my solar plexus about? On my short drive home, I contemplated this feeling: It felt like a slight judgment of my dear friend and colleague. My mind involuntarily jetted over to: I've always found him to be disconnected from his emotions, very performance-driven, in his head, and always in a rush, going full throttle while keeping too many plates spinning in the air. I would never describe this person as one who loves to stop and smell the roses. With that personality, I wondered how he could connect with his clients and their vulnerability. So different from myself. I cry with my clients, am very touchy-feely, and even pride myself on being perfectly present in conversation.

Pointing the finger outside ourselves, just as I was separating myself from him and making his manner wrong, is generally more comfortable than going inward. Still, that comfort comes at the expense of clarity. Carl Jung once observed that "those who look outside themselves dream, but those who look within become enlightened." When we recognize judgment within ourselves toward others, we can interrupt that pattern by widening the gap between trigger and reaction to discover the raw spot underneath. There, we find our ego states suiting up their armor, lest we learn the truth: We rush to judge the other because we see in them something we reject in ourselves. As the adage goes, *I will look within my own heart first, the easiest to see, that the faults I see in others, are really faults in me.* In principle, this is basic cause and effect, but in application, the ego state's shadow moves as fast as lightning.

Initially, the notion that I needed to do a U-turn seemed absurd. But I wondered: *Was there a part that resided in my shadow self that felt too threatening for me to connect and get acquainted with? Could I be disowning my shadow self, staying safe from a part within me I found despicable or shame-filled, by projecting onto him and then judging him for it? So, where am I disconnected emotionally? Maybe not with my clients, but was I disconnected from my husband, pets, the environment, the animals I eat, myself???*

Maybe that was it. . . maybe I was disconnected from the animals I eat as part of my regular diet! Just the day before this encounter with my colleague, I had a three-hour mini-intensive session with an out-of-town client, who at the end of the session somehow got on the topic of him choosing to be a vegetarian at times and how good it made him feel—more enlightened. I shared that while I had tried several times to convert because it felt like the right thing to do, I had failed miserably. I expressed a desire to give it another try because when I stop and contemplate the all-too-common farming practices, I find it disturbing, and it sends me into a crisis of conscience! I mean, we don't really need to kill animals *inhumanely* to nourish our bodies.

My curiosity was piqued with this inward journey

and, I entertained another possible area of disconnect—my marriage. I recalled a conversation my husband and I have shared many times. I complain that he watches too much TV. He replies that he feels disconnected when I walk in the door after work, and I'm still on a call with a client or friend. In that, I'm ignoring him (apparently, I have done this a lot, which is why I have been uber aware of it lately and finished up my calls prior to entering the house). He also comments how at times when he's trying to tell me something, I will be on my phone texting a client or friend. And both he and my brother have accused me of stacking my schedule too high and zipping from one thing to another, pointing out that I can't just "be in the moment." *Ugh.* Can you see where this is going?

Our time and energy spent pointing fingers at the other for being messy, stingy, annoying, disconnected, self-centered, or wrong could be misdirected. And the power to redirect our energy lies within us. Peter Gärdenfors, Ph.D., a behavioral psychologist, writes about our tendency to get things wrong and make the story up as we go along in *Psychology Today*. He says: "Everything you see, hear, and feel is a magical performance created by your brain. . . [This is] how conscious experiences are generated. The brain, therefore, goes beyond just filling in the blanks - it can also simulate that which does not exist." He refers to our illusion of having the full picture of events in our lives, when our brains are constantly filling in gaps with our default programming. As novelist, Anais Nin, puts it, "We do not see the world the way the world is, we see the world the way we are." We have the power to redirect our energy and the freedom to direct it toward unpacking our shadow, not judging the other.

The reframe of influence going out(other)-in(self) to the direction of in(self)-out(other) removes us from being powerless to the whims of our imprints and into a place of control and power over our thoughts and experiences. My U-turn of introspection allowed me to extend compassion to myself and, in turn, compassion to my friend. The knot in my stomach softened, I immediately felt lighter, and the "constriction" in my body lessened.

However, if we continue living in the land of projecting our shadow self out there, onto the other to eradicate it from ourselves, we keep ourselves disconnected from our deepest raw spots that hold boundless treasures. Jung wrote in his journals that "The shadow is ninety percent gold," referring to our repressed subconscious beliefs. Jungian analyst John Sanford goes a step further and posits that evil isn't in the shadow but in the ego's need to repress it, as he explains with D. Patrick Miller for *The Sun*. Sanford says:

> Whatever has been repressed holds a tremendous amount of energy, with a great positive potential. So, the shadow, no matter how troublesome it may be, is not intrinsically evil. The ego, in its refusal of insight and its refusal to accept the entire personality, contributes much more to evil than the shadow.

Consider that the "bad" thing that happens when we criticize others may not be their actions but instead how our ego builds itself up to bully a shadow into staying hidden.

There is a shorter way than my example to connect directly with healing the self and resetting the narrative. Instead of others' actions being triggers for us that pull us under into default patterns of defensiveness, now we can see those triggers as grist for the mill. Ask yourself: *How is what I see that I dislike on some level true about me?* Yes—That's the ticket! Continue to ask questions that invite us into increasingly complex levels of self-awareness. There, we may even choose to love that which we dislike or are offended by in others.

In *Getting the Love You Want*, Harville Hendrix, PhD, refers to the science of attachment, suggesting that the quickest track to fully integrating the self is to love what we hate in the other. When I offer Harville's insight to clients as a remedy for the relationship aches that ail them, I'm met with a variety of responses: confusion, disgust (love what I hate in the other?), and curiosity. Next, they resist. Loving the other and what we view in them as wrong requires that we love the disowned part of ourselves that we had to deny to keep the attachment framework going. Hence, we unearth parts of ourselves that feel too threatening to love on, submerged in the subconscious. This quick—yet difficult—step is available to all of us at any time. Still, most of us require the scenic route in our discovery, healing, and integration of self to develop a wide enough lens to know there's nothing to forgive.

THEY ARE BOTH LIES. . . A
CAUTIONARY TALE ON FALSE SELVES
AND AUTHENTIC SELVES. . .

Throughout my life, conflicting encounters have sent me to this place of quandary: *How is it that some seem to dislike me so much while others sing my praises? After all, am I not the common denominator?* I have mulled and mulled over the dichotomy that I've felt rejected over what seemed to be no good reason, while so many others throughout my life have sung my praises. They've even given me more credit than I deserve, describing me as having a confident and self-assured presence when I walk into the room, saying that my energy and aura shine brighter than most others (something I didn't fully believe). Those opposing views shaped my conflicting inner world.

At different times in my life, I have leaned on wise counsel to help me decipher who was right about me or on which side of the riddle I should finally settle—until about fourteen years ago. A friend stopped my line of questioning cold. She looked me right in the eyes and said, "They're both lies."

They're both lies? You mean, I don't have to choose one over the other? And if I don't have to choose, I pondered quietly, then what do I choose? This struck a chord of truth so deep in my being that it instantly shifted how I view all sides of messages from others. I no longer identify with words of praise, nor words that feel like judgment. I realize both say more about them than about me, anyway.

We do well not to allow the pendulum to swing from "I'm unworthy" to "I'm the greatest person who has ever lived." Both cognitions pull us left or right of center; in the middle, we find the truest view of the self. The Tao Te Ching alludes to this in its teaching on how inflating our ego can be as destructive as self-negativity; just like going up or down a ladder, both movements are unstable: Success is as dangerous as failure. This principle invites us to shed views of others and integrate a widened view of self. Doing so increases our capacity to forgive things we've taken personally and positions us to focus on the next step of the NPP, which is reframing our view of the other.

POINTS OF CONTEMPLATION

Through integration, we learn lessons from the past, which inform our future actions. The questions below will help you develop a truer view of self, so you can be a better version of you.

- Think of a future event that is causing you some distress. What NC best describes the nature of that concern? Rewrite that statement in the positive, reflecting how you would like to feel about yourself in that situation. Example: "I'm unworthy" might become "I'm good enough, even with my flaws."

- Close your eyes and walk through that scene, holding the frame of how you would like to feel about yourself at that moment. What feels different? How do you feel, sound, and act?

- Reflect on your family tree and list any themes that run through it. What issues seem to cascade from one generation to the next? What dysfunctional patterns impact you and will most likely impact future generations if not healed now?

- List the traits in others that tend to get under your skin. The ones you find most irritating.

- Making a U-turn, sit with the following question: how, in any way, is this true about me? What bubbles up for you?

- Choose a time when someone showered you with praise that puffed up your ego and left you feeling, well, just a little bit better about yourself. What danger do you see in allowing your ego to be stroked, even by positive words?

CHAPTER 6

Widening the Lens: View of The Other

"Having compassion for the self, we reconcile all beings in the world."

TAO TE CHING—LAO TZU

After our integration work is well underway, the days of throwing ourselves on the sword to hold connection with others (or being perplexed by relentless relational themes) are much fewer. We're not on the end of life's whipping stick anymore, feeling victimized by the old narratives swirling in our minds. Sure, we still reside in the same physical body, but we have a new perspective, offering our hearts and minds the opportunity of a new, more authentic view of ourselves and others.

If the goal in picking up this book was to relieve suffering or to grow in wisdom, then our work is still incomplete. Widening our view of others is just as paramount to investigate as our view of self. We now have more space in our being to offer up some compassion instead of the old patterns of restriction, which were born out of false beliefs that we are now integrating. Maybe the person behind me isn't just a grumpy man driving recklessly in a big SUV who flipped me off for pulling out in front of him. Perhaps, instead, he's in a rental car he just picked up near the airport, having just flown in from the other side of the country to visit his mother, who is in the ICU on life support. He's not a jerk. He's overwhelmed, scared, lost, sad, and uncertain about whether he will get a chance to say goodbye. What if we gave everyone this Get Out of Jail Free card? Am I letting him off the hook? Does that even matter if I experience a different domain of existence in which his expression of road rage doesn't affect me? Well, the answer is yes, and let's look at why.

Widening our lens to include the view of the other is possible when we tolerate our emotional states and abandon our defense mechanisms. Struggles with this process are normal and usually point to additional raw spots to further heal; the more we heal, the less need we feel to hold grievances against others. This openness invites us to be curious instead of assuming their worst intentions. We may begin to see that they, too, wear false selves and can be ruled by their shadow selves, born of old wounds and distorted self-views. Developing compassion and seeing the other in a new light becomes realistic as we do this inner work. And it emanates from us to bless others, too.

WHY WE STRUGGLE TO WIDEN THE LENS

Over dinner recently, I shared this writing project with some friends. As soon as I introduced the title, *It's Never Personal*, a debate of cataclysmic proportions launched from the other side of the table. My friend's husband gasped and said, "How dare you say it's not personal when the person looked me square in the eye and said, 'you're not a valuable member of our team, and we have to let you go?" Few topics rattle people's cages more than telling them that something wasn't personal when they "know" it was. And I get it. He was feeling psychological whiplash from a raw spot. And doesn't he have a point?

What about when a parent looked you straight in the eye and said "Get the fuck out of my face. The sight of you makes me sick!" My father actually said this to me when I was thirty-five, and I was deeply hurt. Some wounds cut us to the bone. They feel so personal that we may not initially want to let the other off the hook, seeming to condone their "bad" behavior. Well, that's fair enough. After all, reconciling someone's harsh words may seem nearly impossible when our inner child still requires peace. A short time later, I learned that when my father said those words to me, undiagnosed cancer was spreading throughout his body. Perhaps he had something going on physiologically, and that possibility allowed me to stop wondering, *How could he say that to his daughter?* Likewise, many of my clients recount vicious words a parent said, but instead of turning the finger toward self-contempt like I had, they look outward with a contemptuous eye to the other.

Let's face a tough truth. When we're hurting, we cast "the other" as the enemy of our hearts and our hurt. We're so accustomed to placing the blame "out there" that we'll naturally cling to wanting someone to pay for the injustice or the heartache. However, we deceive ourselves when we allow the "gut reaction" or somatic discomfort to dictate our view of the other as a perpetrator and us the victim. Within the gap between trigger and response, we may override our automatic reactions and access free will to forge a new response. There, we discover the option to enlist higher wisdom and powers of reasoning to incorporate a view of the other that serves the greater good, us and them. That path of forgiveness frees us from a need for justice and meaningfully soothes the raw spot.

As clients walk with me this far, they begin imagining that they can interpret others' words and intentions differently... then they tend to pause here. Exploring this notion can feel *very* vulnerable, like we're too exposed or fragile. They ask, "If I don't have my grievance, then what?" Well, what if the grievance no longer had power over you or the way you feel? What feels so scary about releasing that grievance? The raw spots those grievances occupy may become places in the heart, mind, and body that no longer hold an emotional charge—or a much weaker one – and open some level of spaciousness for warm feelings to move in. *Your feelings could hurt a whole lot less.*

As with my dad's hurtful statements, sometimes that wound is still triggered, yet less and less with time. There are still times my mind wanders off from the events of that day, and I'm once again seduced by the old narrative of "I'm unlovable." Today, that translates to asking, *What flaw could exist in me that would cause a father to say that to his daughter?* Painful memories have alluring aspects: a part of our psyche wants to relive the pain and gets pulled in again. This seeming gravitational pull is not to be judged; instead, view it as a normal part of the process. Having done the work in this book, I don't stay stuck in the endless circuitous spiral of taking it personally, feeling heaviness in the heart, burdened by the feelings of sadness, and caught and swept up by the tumbleweed of thinking I am not lovable. Without the grievance, I can reassure my inner child and remind her she is loved and loveable—and she knows it. However, this degree of healing requires me to reframe my grievance with my father about what he said to me so many years ago.

Almost mysteriously, when we change our view of self, paradigm shifts occur in our interpretation of past events. Yes, even our realities of past events change. After all, as I mention in the last chapter, our view of the world isn't the whole picture; that view shows us the world "the way we are." So, we change ourselves—our position—and everything we see shifts. Reframing painful past experiences requires us to widen our lens to shift how we view the other. This becomes possible when we let go of our certainty about the past and become curious about what else might be true.

WIDENING THE LENS

"I. Don't. Know." An important component of not taking things personally is having the wisdom to say, "I don't know." Or at least open the door to *maybe* not knowing. This allows us to explore the world from a place of curiosity and wonder, and non-judgment, versus being stuck in the world of identification with the egoic self and pride, which has a tone of "I already have all the answers." Believing we have the answers and assuming certain beliefs to be fact is like looking through a microscope and thinking you see the whole world. But you're missing all the other possibilities beyond our myopic view. Attachment to a single perspective is often what Proverbs 16:18 describes as "the pride before the fall." How do we avoid the fall? By stepping back from the microscope and widening our lens. This vantage point appeals to our higher-minded and wiser self, leading us to seek a better-informed truth: truth that is more aligned with God's truth, universal wisdom, and what the Taoist refer to as the Tao.

We don't and can't access universal wisdom when we believe our ideas are sacred truths. Why? Because we're putting ourselves on the holy throne, as if we already contain all knowledge. *Spoiler alert: We don't.* The apostle Paul speaks to this in 2 Corinthians 10:5: "We demolish arguments and every pretension that sets itself up against the knowledge of God, and we take captive every thought to make it obedient to Christ." Bottom line is, the one who says, "I know" has already demonstrated a lack of objectivity, and two words are rife with the potential of "the pride before the fall."

Consider that throughout history, scientists, philosophers, and poets alike clung to the theory that the earth was flat and at the center of the universe. This one-sided certainty closed off the possibility of another reality. Some were so threatened by the 'round earth' concept that anyone espousing it was imprisoned or executed. Needless to say, eventually, the tide turned against the long-held and fought-for flat earth theory; it fell alongside Greek gods like Atlas, the famous Titan, thought to hold the entire universe in the form of a globe in his hands.

Why? Because Galileo, an astronomer, physicist, and engineer during the Italian Renaissance, didn't cling to existing constructs. That would have kept him stuck believing the world was flat and at the center of the universe. Instead, he sat in the I-don't-know and dispelled the theory that the earth was the center of the universe and made several other interplanetary discoveries. As result, he's considered "the father of modern science – all for sitting in lap of curiosity and open-mindedness.

Sitting in the I-don't-know has allowed some of the greatest minds in the history of humanity to reach new heights of discovery and truth. With each new fact, we widen our lens to see more of what's true and real in the world. Applied to our healing journeys, we can view widening the lens with a sense of wonder, rather than fear and dread. Be like Galileo and be open to new ideas instead of being closed to them.

For example, a couple, we'll call them Terra and Brian, was seeing me for couples counseling because they wanted to understand and take control of their pattern of arguments that pushed each other away and instead achieve greater intimacy. They felt powerless over these scenes, which left them both feeling alone, confused, and hopeless. In one session, the husband described an incident from the night. He had shared with Terra his vulnerable place of not feeling important and cared for and not feeling understood emotionally in the relationship. She immediately changed the subject and began discussing finances, so he became quiet and withdrawn. She noticed this shift and interpreted that 'it's all about sex with him, and if he doesn't get it, then he gets upset.' Terra blamed herself for not being sexually available enough and thus pushing him away and causing his bad mood—the same pattern her mother complained about with her father.

Brian was surprised by her comment, and after observing the look on his face, I asked him if she was correct in her assessment. He shared a whole side of him that shuts down when he wants to feel more important to her and cannot achieve it. This new information widened Terra's lens and showed her that what she assumed he was thinking and feeling wasn't true—this huge miss was typical within their cycle of frustration and disconnection. Notice how quickly our lens can narrow, and the myopic view sets in. Not seeing the full picture can lead to "mis-attunement" in interpersonal relationships, and repair is only possible when we slow our quick judgments down and get out of a reactive stance. This allows us to access our higher executive awareness to discover what we don't know that may be true.

You may wonder how this ties into not taking things personally. That depends. Are you content looking through a narrow lens, where judgment is distorted, so views of self and others are skewed, leading to decisions based on poor information? Probably not. But despite our intentions, we make assumptions about others that are mostly wrong, based on our attachment frames and scripts from our family of origin—all to keep us safe from discomfort or pain. Remember, we have a bent towards assuming and avoiding negativity. It's about survival here!

What if, instead of taking Brian's silence as criticism of her, Terra was vulnerable and asked him to tell her what was going on—thus giving him the attention he wanted? Doing so requires Terra to avoid her default assumption that she caused his pain, putting her in a defensive position. Instead, she can be curious and open—emotionally available. (If she wishes to, she can use the generational clearing tools from Chapter 5 to revisit whether something else might've also been true in her parents' relationship).

I believe that widening of the lens and seeing the other with compassion (to some degree) happens organically, for the most part, when we do our work and grow our emotional tolerance for the stories of others. In a healthy interpersonal relationship, both parties will respond to each other with an "I don't know" attitude, setting us up to explore any situation with curiosity and nonjudgement. But we don't arrive here once and check a box. Lao Tzu speaks to this in the Tao Te Ching, saying, "Every good man is a bad man's teacher. Every bad man is a good man's job. If you do not understand this, you will get lost, however intelligent you are. It is the great secret." Lao Tzu calls on us to embrace humility and a spirit of continuing to learn from one another; today, you're the teacher in a certain interaction, and tomorrow, you're the student. That duality allows us to remain humble in every encounter and every relationship. The 'secret' is to widen your lens and look for more information about what else could also be true.

VIEW OF THE OTHER

In Chapter 1, I introduce the idea of defensive walls of protection that we build around our hearts, which keep us from being vulnerable and connecting with others. Dr. John Conger, author of *The Body in Recovery* and Director of the Institute for Jungian and Reichian Studies, observes that while everyone needs some "armor of protection," therapy seeks not only to dissolve the armor, but to introduce flexibility and conscious choice into an often rigid, unconscious defense structure." This happens as we access our ego states, connect with them spiritually, feel compassion for our broken parts, and bring our false selves' new truths through integration.

As our walls come down, we build emotional tolerance and increase our bandwidth to hold different realities as possibly true. If having walls of protection causes constriction in the body, creating dis-ease, then the opposite holds true; when we're at one with the universal flow, the body returns to a state of ease and good health. Anecdotally, I've seen a woman who released her resentment over an estranged son report that her tension headaches went away, and he came back into her life. Another client forgave his ex-wife for things he blamed her for in their divorce, and this improved intimacy in his current marriage—and his acid reflux hasn't flared up since. With our walls down, lines of communication that have long been constricted (behind our walls and outside of them) now have more space for Qi (energy) to flow. We no longer expend energy upholding walls of defense, and we have more headspace and heart space for joy, ease, and creative pursuits.

As we become conduits for energy to move through us, it flows out onto others. This removes the short-sighted frame from our view, opening our eyes to the brokenness in others—their protective walls, distorted views of self, and the frailty of the human psyche—who need healing in the same ways that we were once pained. But after decades of operating within a certain system of beliefs, such as us/them, good/bad, wrong/right, people have good reasons not to want to see the other as we are: broken, alone, flawed, and in need of redemption. Yet, doing so acknowledges the fuller spectrum of truth we observe with a wider lens. Keeping our walls down to perceive this new awareness, rather than looking away, requires a complete paradigm shift. That can be a foreign and scary notion and requires the groundwork already laid down in the first several chapters.

Having excavated enough of our personal stories, we realize that our view of self, the other, and the entire world are all constructs built by the systems of the egoic mind. Others pick up stories that don't serve them, too. I believe there's no personal history that, if shared by another, wouldn't move most of us to be drawn into our mutual stories that hold the common longings, emptiness, pain, and suffering: we all ache. Everyone has felt the burden of insecurity and loneliness, and at some point has wrestled with what the 16th century Spanish mystic poet, St. John of the Cross, refers to as, the Dark Night of the Soul—a painful period in one's life." Releasing the false parts (both ours and theirs) means *we aren't separate after all.*

During a client's session, he wondered about his ex-fiancé: "If there's no more 'she's bad, I'm good,' what is there?" I cast a vision of the future for him and mentioned that *maybe* at some point in his journey, he may even feel moved to hug her, feeling profound empathy as a fellow human being on this often-jagged road of life. He rejected this idea so strongly that he almost lunged across the room at me. *Ok, not really.* However, what I said is true. Once we see the other as hurting the way we have, we can be drawn into a posture of compassion, humility, and *weeping for the other.* In Romans 12:14-15, the apostle Paul admonishes the Romans to "Bless those who curse you; bless and do not curse. Rejoice with those who rejoice; weep with those who weep." When we don't retaliate and instead act with kindness or share in their sorrow or joy, we open space for the other to show up differently, as you learned in the last chapter.

MOVING TOWARD COMPASSION – REFRAMING THE OTHER

Perhaps no greater story in history speaks inordinately to the notion that nothing, no matter how painful, is personal more so than the story of Jesus on the cross. While being crucified, Jesus cries out, "Forgive them, Father, for they know not what they do." Most of us hear this story and presume that the lesson is solely: forgive; forgive them as we are forgiven. Take a moment and conjure up an image in your mind of a past hurt; a time when you had to dig down deep into the well of forgiveness and pull out a big bucket of, "I forgive you for offending me, hurting me," etc. We're programmed to forgive what the other has done.

But this "forgiveness-for-forgiveness" interpretation ignores the second half of his prayer. Jesus forgives them not for what they did, but for "not knowing" what they were doing. *How could his persecutors not know?* I mean, they were well aware of their false testimonies and actions to have a man executed. But Christ saw that they held a strong conviction regarding their actions; doing so because they were lost in their distorted, false sense of self that they projected onto him. They had forgotten who they are in the spirit, as children of God. When others are lost, we can feel for them instead of passing judgment on them because we were lost at one point also (even more so before we picked up this book. ☺).

With Christian and atheist clients alike, I have yet to meet a person who isn't impacted by the richer meaning of this story that everyone has been lost in our false sense of self; highjacked by a part of our personality that doesn't really belong to us. Essentially, our distorted view of self. We tend to stay with the narrative that we know until we find another vantage point from which to see a situation—people *do* better when we *know* better.

Try reframing ways others have offended us not as: 'I forgive you for what you did,' but 'I forgive you because *you didn't know/ you didn't have a wider lens.*'

What happens when you flip the script? Does it provide a little space to entertain a different perspective? Does that feel more open to your heart, mind, and body? This radical reframe peels back our illusion that what the other has done is "bad" and needs to be forgiven by us. We're invited into the perspective of the mind of Christ to release the judgment we're sitting in. Our lens of right and wrong zooms out of rigidly thinking that there's something to forgive if we're hurt. We release our false self that sat in judgment of the other and release them from their false sense of self, too.

From our new premise, we can rewrite the old narrative with the theme of compassion, not blame. Inner balance is established when we extend compassion to our vulnerable parts and increase our appreciation that all humans have tasted and wrestled with the belief of feeling unworthy or not-enough at some point in our lives. These are among the great equalizers in the human experience, including the fallout from dynamics from our family of origin and trauma. In nature, everything exists on a spectrum, and there's no exception with humans. The degree of our woundedness lies somewhere along a continuum.

Ultimately, our understanding of forgiveness evolves as we evolve. In Chapter 1, we illuminated how so often we bypass much needed work of the self for the sake of connection with the other. Now that we're more integrated, our ego states are balanced, and our adult self is at the helm, we may no longer sacrifice peace for connection. The tools you've learned throughout this book empower us to maintain harmony of worlds within and between that used to perplex us. We also grow in discernment, which allows us to keep the wall around our hearts open, so our interpersonal relationships flow more easily, and we have more freedom of choice, including to maintain healthy boundaries.

DISCERNMENT

A few years ago, I was on a four-day primitive camping trip in the Pacific Northwest. As we headed off the trail on the last day, I noticed a sign that read: "There is no such thing as loving too much, only loving the wrong way." Just when I thought I had heard and read every quote on love from every angle, this one grabbed me. I thought of how many times as a psychotherapist, clients have told me their relationship(s) are strained because of loving too much:

- A husband says his wife overspends because he "loves her so much" that he lets her get away with it

- A mother swears her conflict with her children is that she "loves them so much" and thus never held them accountable for their actions (believing that giving them their freedom with no boundaries was loving)

- A wife's seething resentment has reached a debilitating level because she allows her alcoholic, verbally abusive husband to take her along for the ride on his dysfunctional dynamic of drinking, promising he is going to quit, and then repeating the cycle of abuse.

She tolerates this in the name of love. They all do. Is that love? Or are they 'loving the wrong way?' *Sigh.*

Believing our problems stem from loving the other "too much" leads us to forgive quickly—and as you've learned, that leads to feeling like a victim and holding resentments. That never-ending saga leads us round and round in circles. As the founder of Emotionally Focus Therapy (EFT), Sue Johnson, often said, we're the creators and the victims of our own stories. *Yes, we contribute to the saga.* We don't arrive at "nothing to forgive" through a reckless abandon of our hearts, allowing others to infringe upon us. Don't sacrifice personal safety and inner peace on an altar of compassion.

To remove ourselves from this quagmire, we combine the wisdom of the heart and mind to dispense compassion and forgiveness in the right, *discerning* way. Like a pharmacist compounding a precise dose, we create a delicate balance of harmony within the self and with others through setting and maintaining healthy boundaries. To name a few, these include holding others accountable, not over-giving, and not tolerating destructive patterns. These boundaries and many more like them clear the way for us to move through this life with a heart wide open, pouring out compassion for others even amid their flaws and extending forgiveness when transgressed by others.

With discernment, a wise heart loves *a lot* and *well*—at the same time. Saint Augustine describes this as, "Hate the sin, love the sinner." We read between the lines and have a felt sense of loving the other, but not at the expense of the self. The root word of discernment in Latin is *discernere*, which means "to separate or divide." Discernment draws from a deep well of inner truth and authenticity built from the work in the previous chapters.

Having already connected our heart and mind to bring compassion to our inner child, we can do the same for others. Being more grounded in our being allows us to "separate" or "divide" right action from wrong action in a territory that's often nuanced, like, "I love you, and you really hurt me." Or "I love you, and your actions are forgivable but not excusable. There are consequences." Taking the other to task will feel extremely awkward and uncomfortable for most people who, up until now, have been loving "the wrong way" under the guise of "loving so much." The late Thich Nhat Hahn said, "To love without knowing how to love, wounds the person we love." That wounds us as well.

We must relearn what loving the other *well* entails. Some of us may believe we are loving well, but we base this assessment on our attachment figures. Our role models may have modeled the wrong way to love because they may not have tuned into healthy boundaries and perhaps violated ours. Let's face it: if we still have our inner child and their ego states driving the bus, we can't possibly expect to make wise decisions regarding boundaries. This manifests in our dysfunctional interpersonal relationships. Fortunately, like all our scripts and imprints, we can shift to an understanding and expression of love that helps us show up better for ourselves and the other.

Yes, there's a recipe for properly loving someone. The

NPP sets us up with a solid inner framework to support a discerning eye rooted in the universal flow of love. This lens shows us how to navigate conflicts in healthy ways. Having done the work in the previous chapters, we tend to flow into a state of honoring ourselves and redeeming our stories. I believe, on a metaphysical plane, this can set up the other to do the same—sort of like an invitation extended in spirit, if you will. The other is invited to show up differently, as we best honor their story by holding them accountable to repair the damage and restore the relationship (for trust to return, it needs to be earned through time and demonstration of right behavior by the other). However, this step doesn't require the other's involvement to transform the dynamic.

However, not all invitations are rsvp'd with a "yes." One of the great laws of nature is that when you change one part of a system, the entire system must change. There's no way around it. There are a few potential outcomes, all of which are favorable for the greater good (all involved):

1. With the new boundary (honoring the self) in place, the other must change (stepping into a place of health) to stay in the relationship with the new rules of engagement/new dynamic. They rise to the occasion and step into their own work. This is a gift to the self and the other.

2. If we honor the self with a new boundary and the other doesn't wish to play by the new rules,

they may leave. This may hurt you, but at least you did not dishonor yourself.

3. You may change, and they don't want to leave but continue with the same dynamic, so you may have to say goodbye to that relationship for a while.

Whatever the outcome, as I often tell my clients, *when we change one part of the system, the entire system changes.*

Take, for example, a parent whose child stole money to take his girlfriend to the movies. The parent (assuming that all or most parts of the self are integrated) can lovingly extend compassion for the child's situation and forgive them for betraying the parent's trust. But that doesn't mean the child has earned back the trust. The discerning parent will hold the child accountable, help them consider honest ways of paying for dates, and provide an appropriate pathway to restore trust. If the stealing continues, the parent may face painful choices, as I have seen with families, particularly where addiction is involved. Looking the other way is easy. But being a loving, caring parent means not allowing the child to steal unchecked. This balancing act of moving through life with an open heart and healthy boundaries brings honor to the parent and the child or any relationship you wish to improve.

THE FALSE SUMMIT

"We are all just walking each other home."

RAM DAS

Hikers on the climb up to the summit of Mount Everest, or any other mountain for that matter, will sometimes encounter the point on the trail that *seems* to be the apex. *We have arrived; mission accomplished,* they think. After investing so much training, endurance, perseverance, and hope in the process and the end goal, of course, the moment of reaching the summit is filled with pure exhilaration. Then they look around and realize they've merely reached the false summit (also called a "false peak"). As you may imagine, disillusionment can set in, overlooking how every step they've taken has gotten them this far and proves they can keep going.

This metaphor holds true for those on the path to enlightenment who seek true and lasting freedom from the suffering of taking things personally. From work with couples, quite arguably, the heaviest lifting is at the beginning of treatment. We map out their cycle, access vulnerable parts, and invite each partner to own their contribution to the dynamic by sharing their vulnerable parts. Thus, the clients learn how to hold space for their partners without giving in to the temptations of interrupting, fixing, dismissing, minimizing, or withdrawing. Whew! There's a lot of energy expended to build what us couples therapists call "safety and intimacy." That translates into significant shifts early on in therapy, as couples learn to reframe their partners as their allies versus their enemies and work together to de-escalate long-standing and oftentimes escalating dynamics. All these key changes lay the groundwork for more profound work yet to be experienced. They move toward becoming masters of repairing mis-attunements.

Just as couples plunge into the recesses of the heart and mind, frequently excavating the crevices that hold areas never touched prior, my individual clients also do the work of this book. After integration is well underway and they go further into cultivating compassion for the other, their lives are profoundly lighter and happier. However, at this point, couples and individuals reach the false summit.

With a mix of apprehension and encouragement, I share a final vision of knowingness with clients at their false summit stage of counseling. In fact, the most profound rich work still lies ahead. What still needs to be done to accomplish their goal—get to the apex? After all, haven't we already excavated the crevices of our hearts and minds to locate those parts that went underground? Was it not the step of integration that brought us into the most congruent parts of ourselves? And now, with our hearts open and having grasped what it means to fully extend compassion to a fellow human being, haven't we arrived at the place we seek? *Not yet.*

POINTS OF CONTEMPLATION

After all your hard work and progress, reaching a false summit can be disheartening—until you see the possibilities of ascending even higher. Use the following questions to discover any lingering resentment that needs the healing of Steps 1-4 of NPP. The more you clear, the more clarity awaits you in Step 5 when you take the birdseye view.

- What's a judgment you have of another person? How firm are you in your conviction of them? Now widen the lens and allow yourself to sit in the "I don't know" about that person. *Maybe what I thought was true about them isn't true after all.* What do you notice in your thoughts? Your body? If this is difficult for you, why might that be?

- Bring into your mind an image of someone whom you had difficulty feeling fond of in the past. Notice their face and say the Hawaiian *Ho'oponopono* prayer to them (aloud or silently). The steps are to say these four things to them seven or eight times:

1. I'm Sorry

2. Please Forgive Me

3. Thank You

4. I Love You

Afterward, journal about what feels different in your thoughts and somatically when you imagine that person.

- Revisit a memory of something you took personally and held against someone, where you now choose "peace and connection in the name of love." Imagine yourself walking through that scene and holding firm, loving boundaries. How does that feel? If you feel any fear or resistance, ask what it represents. Perhaps this is an invitation to revisit a previous step in the process.

- False Summit—How do you feel at this signpost on the journey? Jot down any memories or feelings that still need your attention.

CHAPTER 7

Birdseye View

Out beyond ideas

Of wrongdoing and right doing

There is a field.

I will meet you there.

When the soul lies down

in that grass,

the world is too full

to talk about.

Idea, language

Even the phrase 'each other'

Doesn't make any sense.

—RUMI

THE APEX

The universe is always moving us to a place of homeostasis. Sometimes, the invitation comes as a gentle nudge; other times, the message takes the shape of an avalanche crashing upon our lives. Regardless of the path, the cosmic agenda is always in cahoots with our subconscious agenda: to experience the fullness of who we are. This fullness is waiting for each of us beneath the very roots of taking things personally, separating us from ourselves and others, as you learned in Chapter 1 of this book.

You've learned how to identify the raw spots, shed parts of your personalities that picked up distorted beliefs about the self that didn't serve you, move through this process of peeling back layers of protection, and integrate parts of the self. After learning to hold and release burdened emotions, we see ourselves and others with compassion and discernment. And yet, you may notice confusion or resentment bubbling up as you read this chapter. If that happens, be curious about what that part needs to keep moving toward the summit. Does that part hold a fear that prevents you from making the final climb? Discover what previous step you need to go back to and explore with a sense of curiosity and non-judgment. These detours and doing the work to move through them to continue the climb mean you're on the right track.

The journey of enlightenment through this book provides a roadmap to help us *remember what we have forgotten:* the truth of who we are as individuals and in our relationship with the other. We shift from seeing the other as "over there" and judging ways they're different from us to seeing that the only thing that separates us is our mind and the constructs we create. As we zoom further away from the systems in which our minds tangled us, we move toward the birdseye view: a place few soar. In this place of transcendence, we reach the true summit, the perspective that transcends all egoic thoughts. We no longer view people or situations as good or bad but as "just is." This allows us to accept reality and remain calm no matter what life brings. *What is... Is.*

The place of true freedom from taking things personally resides in the perspective of non-dualistic thinking—the place beyond judgments. The idea of non-dualistic thinking has its roots in both philosophical and spiritual arenas, stretching our ideas of being separate in this plain of existence. Sitting in the seat of compassion for all creation, we see that we're not separate after all. This awareness allows us to experience more joy, untethered to the things we once took personally.

Considering the non-dualistic state of being, I picture the Buddha laughing. He gets the joke. Having transcended all ego states and no longer bound by mental constructs, he sits back and muses that *separation is an illusion.* Fortunately, as Richard Rohr, the founder of The Center for Action and Contemplation, points out: "You don't have to go to a monastery to be a mystic. Living as a mystic means orienting the whole of yourself toward the sacred. It's a matter of purposely looking through the lens of love." In this chapter, you'll discover how to rest in knowing that the universe is unfolding exactly as it should, and from that perspective, trust that things are happening for you, not to you. You'll have the tools and resilience to embrace the ongoing idea that there is nothing to forgive.

THE BIRDSEYE VIEW STATE OF MIND

The first time I considered the freedom of a non-duality view, I was in my second year of my master's program taking a class on Healing Metaphors. It took us to new realms of perspective both intra-personally and inter-personally. In one assignment, we were placed in a small breakout group with two other classmates to each share which animal we would choose to be if we could: our spirit animal, if you will. When it was my opportunity to share, without hesitation, I said, "An eagle."

My group asked, "An eagle? Why an eagle?"

Isn't it obvious?, I thought. In our physical world, who has a fuller vantage point than the birds, the creatures who can claim the title of being the oldest dynasty in the world? They have the greatest view, which for me means they possess the widest lens: the panoramic view. No other animal has their perspective, which affords them certain advantages.

Perhaps we have something to learn from birds, both in metaphor and practical application. In many ways, these creatures with their small reptilian brains surpass our ideas of them as no more than colorful, feathered creatures entertaining us with a glimpse here and a song there. Consider that their sole purpose is to figure out how to live another day. They wildly, organically, and effortlessly seem to keep in sync with the pulse of the universe. (*The pulse of the universe*; those words prompt a sense of a profound experience to wash over me, and I want to taste it. Don't you?).

For example, several years ago in Tennessee, an

entire migratory flock of gold-winged warblers avoided a devastating storm because they detected infrasound waves alerting them to flee their U.S. breeding grounds. These birds received those signals five days in advance *from 900 km away.* Unfortunately, our fellow humans had no such intuition and were unprepared for the ensuing 84 tornadoes that resulted in 35 deaths and tremendous damage. while birds exhibit a knowing in sync with nature's heartbeat, humans are lost in our egoic constructs, following the weather channel as it changes predictions moment to moment.

The birdseye view offers discernment of how everything in the world, including ourselves and those we feel have wronged us, is manifested from the universe's creative expression. We perceive our oneness with all of creation. This clarity helps us harmonize with the inevitable ebbs and flows of life because we understand we're part of a bigger picture. In I Kings 4:29-34, the Bible recounts the story of God offering King Solomon anything he wanted. He could've chosen riches, power, or anything... and he asked for wisdom because he knew he'd be a better ruler with God's sight than just his own.

Enlightenment helps us avoid rushing to judgment or dwelling on the past to live in harmony with "what is" and find peace no matter our circumstances. This perspective gives us wings to soar to new heights on our journey to forgiveness. As I often say to clients progressing to this summit: "To know all is to forgive all." I like to plant this seed to gauge where they are in their journey. I sit and wait for their response.

"But I don't know all," is the usual reply I receive.

Between the lines of their response, I sense a desire to experience this state of "knowing." They connect with a part of their being that wishes to soar higher, where 'only angels seem to tread.' I sense that their curiosity is piqued as they contemplate: *I want to know all, but I don't. Is that even possible? How might I do this? It feels like a huge leap.*

"Yes," I say, "but there's a place within you that has the 'knowing' and may step outside of the thinking mind." Previous chapters of this book illustrate that distortions and illusions are born and reside in the mind (the consequences of such mental constructs showing up in our unsettled spirits and constricted energies). However, we also have a knowing part of ourselves that has never been blemished by words cast onto us by attachment figures. That place within us can never be injured. It's considered the seat of the soul, the mindful one, the observer, the changeless, the mind of Christ. And it resides within you. Yes, you.

All people have access to this changeless part of ourselves. But in our Western culture, where operating from a "cognitive" posture is celebrated, the thinking mind's limited lens almost always blocks us from attaining our sense of knowing. Thus, we're separated from universal wisdom, losing sight of our birthright of oneness with God, others, and ourselves. In our forgetting, we rely on our executive functions to make sense of the world, and as result, we constantly find ourselves unable to forgive. The path to forgiveness is to remember what we've forgotten.

In our most purely innocent (pre-egoic) states, we

knew and felt our interconnection with the universe—
our bodies and minds pulsating with the vibration. To
find our knowing, we must transcend our mental constructs and remember how to tune into that frequency. As
we finally experience our knowing part, we're untethered
from our programmed ways of thinking and can attain
the birdseye view state of mind.

Christian missionary Daniel Everett largely achieved
his deprogramming by accident. He wanted to bring the
hope of the gospel—the new way of thinking—to the
indigenous Pirahã people in the Amazon. Their 350 members were largely isolated from industrialized civilization
with its modern forms and systems, influencers, and
status seeking. Everett spent almost a decade immersed
in the Pirahã culture to teach them the concepts of no
fear of death, nonjudgement, true happiness, and other
enlightened principles. He was surprised that the evidence he accumulated in Bible studies, his prayers, and
his walk as a Christian and a missionary (essentially all
the constructs he had been taught) didn't "hold up to the
evidentiary requirements of this group." He taught them
not to be afraid of dying, but they were already not afraid
of death. He tried to speak to them about judgment. Well,
they didn't know about judgment.

In fact, in this culture, there was no concept of God.
No concept of God? This further baffled Everett because
when he tried to teach them to be happy, again, he came
up empty-handed. How could you be happy without God?
He invited researchers from MIT to help him understand
this culture. The researcher observed that the Pirahã
must be the happiest people on earth, measured by the

"time they spent smiling and laughing." This Amazonian culture doesn't have our binary fears and preoccupations, instead remaining closer to the pulse of nature, where they effortlessly experience harmony and joy.

Author and physician Larry Dossey writes, "To ask that we go beyond this kind of 'either-or' way of thinking seems an invitation to a primitive form of thought that does not square with the potential of the modern age." However, by returning to our 'knowing, we recover the wisdom the Pirahã people demonstrate. When we stop judging, there's nothing to forgive, and we find something that eludes much of our modern society—our expansive capacity for happiness.

WE DON'T HAVE TO WAIT UNTIL THE END TO SOAR HIGHER

I've always heard that when the soul is about to be torn from the body at the moment of death, we're forced into states of consciousness that we never held before. Then, I witnessed this through my mother. She was in the ICU, with all signs pointing to the possibility that this was her last stay there. In the most vulnerable state possible, with a ventilator lodged down her throat, she motioned that she wanted to write something, so I fetched pen and paper. You don't stop to blink an eye in these moments. As I waited on the edge of her hospital bed with anxious anticipation at what she would share, I watched her attempt to write a message. In the most weakened state, but with the strength of will and determination to get her message across, my mother wrote a question in barely legible penmanship.

I couldn't make out what exactly it said immediately, and we went back and forth (both of us frustrated: her for trying to be understood and me for desperately wanting to understand). Finally, we landed on what she was asking: "*Voy a morir*?" Or "am I going to die?" This moment is one of the great equalizers for all of us, and as we say in Spain, death is "the trip that we will all eventually take." It has a way of shedding parts of the egoic mind that we identify with our whole life.

Amongst many existential crises she must've wrestled with during those days was a secret she had held onto since the age of 6. We tend to cling to these secrets out of fear—and because we're terrified of the unknown result if we share them. At the end of my mother's life, she no longer felt a need to expend energy to keep her system of ego states erect to feel perfectly and psychologically intact—to feel safe. This allowed her to tear down a wall she once felt her survival depended on. Over the next few days, after they removed the ventilator, she appeared to effortlessly release that part into the great nebula by sharing a vulnerable part of the self–her shame-filled secret. At the end of her life, she must have become acutely aware that her need to cling to the wall had been an illusion.

All the danger my mother believed that wall protected her from was invented by her mental programming. As children, we often learn what things to say to be rewarded and which get us punished, and these distinctions can be very real and true in that context. But years later in the larger world. . . the ego states, held so tightly in place, also become illusions as their need dissipates, like we're stationing lifeguards in a desert.

I'm reminded of the parable of Saint Peter and the man who lived on the Isle of Crete who requested to be buried with a handful of soil from the field he lovingly tended. He arrived, fists clenching soil, outside the pearly gates, and Saint Peter told him he needed to let go of that dirt to pass into the gates of heaven. The man refused and sat outside the gates, waiting and waiting. Finally, a little girl came outside and offered him her hand, and he took it, and the soil spilled out. Together, they walked through the gates. Inside, he saw his beloved isle of Crete amongst even more splendor. Reflecting on this story, if my mother had let go of her wall sooner, might that have been the very action that would lead her to the desired safety that made her reinforce the wall?

Die before you die, right? In the final separation, our body will be ripped away from the soul. This realization is succinctly summed up in the Netflix series, *The Kaminsky Method,* by Michael Douglas's character. He describes waking up to the reality of death as a moment filled with "disbelief and wonder."

Do I sound morbid? I bring this up because reframing mortality can be a powerful tool for releasing past hurts and accessing deeper truths. While nothing will force the widening of the lens faster and with more drastic precision than our mortality, we don't have to wait for that experience to soar to new heights in consciousness and freedom.

ATTAINING A SENSE OF WHOLENESS

Think of a time when you were in judgment of someone. How did you feel physically? Emotionally? Were your thoughts all over the place, or was your mind calm? Soon after my officemates betrayed me, I felt disjointed in my being: feeling one thing (somatic disturbance – heaviness in my heart or tension in my solar plexus), thinking another (I am bad, they are good or vice versa), and at times finding that my outward expression didn't line up with my thoughts or feelings. I portrayed "Everything is fine. Nothing to see here," betraying my inner turmoil. This incongruency between and within heart-mind-body kept my energy tied up: I vacillated between modes of self-deprecation (am I so flawed as to evoke this level of contempt from another human being?) and judgment toward the other (she's got issues, obviously!), all in the name of self-protection. With my emotional pendulum swinging from trying to reward the good to punishing the bad, peace and calm were unattainable or fleeting.

In other stories of betrayal in my life, I would extend too much compassion and sacrifice my tender spots that first needed tending to, feeling like a martyr. Ignoring my hurt and "sucking it up" was no more successful than stoking my anger, in terms of forgiveness. We're not in a forgiving state of being when our body, mind, and spirit aren't aligned. Each time we need to forgive someone, we must first bring ourselves into wholeness again.

After connecting with my inner child and holding a lot of my vulnerability, I regained congruence in my heart, mind, and body. I could think about the same people and retain a sense of harmony, wholeness, and alignment. A part of me even grew to see past their physical form and witness the spirit behind it: their broken, beautiful humanness brimming with fear and needing their own story of redemption. In this process, I also better honored my spirit, tapping into a newfound sense of authenticity, freeing up even more parts of my being to a lightness of spirit. I experienced a genuinely open heart from which I could pour love, acceptance, and peace onto others: John C. Pierrakos describes this as ". . . the hum of emotion, the pulse of love." Through this lens, more and more, I saw others not as separate from me but as one mind and heart, though we're in separate bodies.

I've felt rejected plenty of times, both before the incident with my colleagues and after I found peace with them in my being. In every instance, I felt the old familiar trigger, but each time felt different. Those new dings were burning off leftover false selves and distortions of others, like the process of heating iron to release the impurities and create a stronger metal—steel. Not that I've reached a place of enlightenment absent of triggers, but through the steps in this book, I've healed my nervous system enough to feel different in my body, heart, and mind, becoming less and less triggered by others. Experiences I used to feel as sharp-edged are now blunted to dull sensations that invite me more into curiosity versus reaction. In situations I once would've felt hurt, sometimes my gut response is now compassion.

Our unconscious agendas seem to be in a never-ending dance of giving and receiving messages with others, for the mutually beneficial and sole purpose of growing in consciousness. Becoming the most whole versions of ourselves requires the fullest expression of our being; the heart won't settle for cheap substitutes. As we engage in this ongoing communication dance through the birdseye view, we grow in consciousness, revealing more freedom of choice and less suffering for ourselves and others. As John C. Pierrakos states:

> In health, which is the good or truth of life, the reality of the human being, energy and consciousness are very much unified. Man feels this unity. When man is in a healthy state, his life is in a constant creative process. He is inundated with feelings of love, of oneness with other human beings. The oneness is the awareness that he is not different from others. He wants to help them; he identifies with them; he senses that anything that is happening to them, is happening to himself.

So, go ahead and breathe a sigh of relief. Know that you're not alone in your suffering; we're all in this together. Yes, even the ones in the spotlight who seem to have all the answers and portray themselves as being fully self-assured and flawless—them too. *Aaah.* That feels incredible, doesn't it?

BEYOND EGO STATES — THERE IS NOTHING TO FORGIVE

The illusion of separation between ourselves and others points to the 4-10-second gap between subconscious choice and active response mentioned in Chapter 4. Since you reached this point in the book, you're walking a path most are unaware of. The old ways of forgiving, which often involve a thin veneer of niceness on the surface but leave us sometimes seething with a lingering resentment, are stuck in the automatic of our thoughts. At a birdseye view, we see that most thoughts we depend on contain a microscopic speck of the available information, and the gap between trigger and action is a panorama of wisdom and knowledge. This points to an all-encompassing view of forgiveness within the reach of all who desire true freedom from the shackles that bind us when we take things personally.

I believe the humbling recognition that *there is nothing to forgive, and it was never personal*, is the highest summit of spiritual evolution. A meek position awaits us at this peak because we become free of ego and pride there. On this topic, The Course in Miracles states, "To understand the freedom that is available to us in this domain, we need to first understand it's elucidation." When a raw spot is triggered, by default, we fall into ego patterns of reacting, withdrawing, rushing to forgive, or perhaps throwing up impenetrable walls of protection. However, zooming out and shifting to the birdseye view, we see that our wall-building ego, as was stated in my graduate program, refers to the binary **sinners sinned against** paradigm. When we drop a judgment, our ego removes the corresponding wall.

So long as a part of our personality structure is building a story about an injustice or an offense, inevitably, we uncover another egoic state suggesting we must forgive someone for something. Each ego state represents a construct that keeps us in the illusion of separation. A simple and relatable example for all of us is the friend who makes a comment in a casual conversation that rubs you the wrong way: they say watching sports is lazy. Your feelings are *hurt* because you and your husband watch sports, and you're enjoying a well-deserved respite from a busy work week. This immediately pulls you into having a slight that needs to be forgiven, setting up a never-ending and exhausting cycle. There is a better way—higher ground. We go high by leveling the ego wall that creates the story that they committed an offense, and we are offended. With a widened lens, we attain higher ground more easily as we give others the benefit of the doubt. We let people off the hook because we know they're probably driven by their autopilot programming and were completely unaware of what happened. We could imagine that the person commenting about football had a father who often said, "Watching sports is lazy." That script is written into her soul's tapestry, and she repeats it without knowing why. If she stopped to reflect, she could realize she doesn't even believe it herself.

Our egos can be tricky to tease out because the wall feels tied to a part of you—your identity. Identifications with ego states are so powerful because they have survival drives with embedded lessons for both the sender and receiver. What if when the friend denigrates watching sports, instead of being offended as a sports fan, we wonder why? Or we let their words run past us like water flowing down a stream? No ego wall either way. We're not upset with our friend, and our mind avoids a narrative of "How dare they say that?" that could last for days, weeks, or even longer. I've recalled comments from others that glommed onto me and stayed lodged in a crevice in my mind sometimes for years. That is, until I learned a higher way.

As we peel back overidentification with our perceived identities, including walls of protection and separation between ourselves and others, our increasing wholeness negates the entire narrative based on offenses. We're no longer the victim, and therefore, the other isn't the perpetrator. So, we no longer feel a need to counterbalance behavior of others with forgiveness—there's no offense and no offender to forgive. This is experiencing nothing to forgive.

Stepping into nothing-to-forgive requires us to move from "ego manifestation" to "spirit manifestation" by completing the previous steps in this book and communing with the true self, the one in line with the Universe. Here, we experience the zero gravity of non-duality, finding the oneness, the nothingness, and the everything. We perceive that everything we thought was real, hurtful, and sinful was invented by our mental programming. We don't see others as separate beings trying to hurt us, but rather as ourselves—as conduits of the universe's beauty, magnificence, and energy that's always looking for a way to come into being and manifest in the world.

Are you thinking this seems a bit lofty and idealistic? *Well, you're right.* You're probably like most people on the forgiveness journey. Few reach the birdseye view, and almost none achieve it as a lifestyle. But when we stay tuned in to moving from ego to spirit, we catch glimpses of our knowing. Yes, glimpses. At best, we climb through the ego and reach our spirit, recharging our souls with the full view of our congruency and connection with all creation—only to be plucked down by yet another trigger on planet Earth.

"We lose ourselves but find a universe."

HUMANS TRANSCENDING

"Nothing to forgive" doesn't imply that we are no longer human, with real emotions, needing to mourn losses, grieve betrayals, weep, and navigate the forgiveness process. By choice, nothing-to-forgive is a summit we can aim for as we continue navigating the complexities that riddle our human relationships, where we may experience our most painful suffering. We constantly bump up against each other's tender places, the areas still crying out, "Pay attention to me, I still need some healing here." Being human is no easy ride, even under the best of circumstances. The great equalizers across humanity are loss, pain, betrayal, loneliness, rejection, sickness, and death. The nature of human suffering is just as true today as it was when the prophet Kahlil Gibran wrote: "Your pain is the breaking of the shell that encloses your understanding." Yes, we're invited to grow through our ongoing and continued suffering. The pain invites us into the spirit realm.

And yet, not all who suffer become wise. Some become bitter. So, what's the defining factor between those who take one road instead of the other? The differentiator is this: when things happen that trigger us, we may create meaning or judgments about it from the ego—or we may create meaning from the spirit. Looking for "right" and "wrong," we often aim inward, blaming ourselves, or outward, blaming others. Our verdicts seek evidence to incarnate themselves, and that repetition propels us toward bitterness. Or we can seek knowledge to learn and grow from the experience. As our wisdom grows, so do our hearts. We can choose either path. Either way, these stories have meanings about the self, which it tells itself.

Have you seen the same event occur, and two people remember it very differently? I was in the car with my husband a few years ago, and while at a stop light, I noticed a family, parents with a couple children by their side. They were waiting for the light to turn so they could cross four lanes of traffic and enter a shopping center. There was no reason for me to think anything other than *what a sweet, happy-looking family*. And yet, I found the following words spilling out of my mouth: "Gosh, that makes me sad."

My husband replied, "Oh boy, what are you telling yourself about that family?" We both chuckled. He knows me well enough to know that I project meaning onto *others'* stories that frequently don't sync up or exist in reality. Notice I said "others." I tend to see through a lens that assigns a meaning that people are suffering, feeling lonely, or sad. When I run my thought process by others, they often see completely different stories and meanings—because they approach the same information from a worldview that people are happy or resilient. When we assign meanings to stories and events, as authors of our experience, we can interrupt our default programming and choose a new perspective.

Beyond looking for a silver lining, we can frame life's challenges as opportunities for learning and growing. David Hoffmeister discusses framing our difficulties with others through the Holy Spirit Shift: instead of feeling cursed, we can tell ourselves, "I was blessed by this encounter." And WHY does that encounter bless us? Even if our feelings were badly hurt, we lost money or love, or someone else we care about suffered? Hoffmeister says we can still feel blessed because whatever this other person may have done, they showed you an ego state that needs healing.

You've learned in this book how our interpretations of all external events are outside projections of our inward conditions of wounding or healing. What if the next time you feel offended, you consider it's happening *for you,* not to you? As Richard Rohr says:

> Set your intention to uncover the jewels buried in the heart of what already is. Choose to see the face of God in the face of the bus driver and the moody teenager, in peeling a tangerine or feeding the cat. Decide. Mean it. Open your heart, and then do everything you can to keep it open. Light every candle in the room.

After all, we may betray ourselves, and others may betray us, but the universe, in all its wisdom, will never betray us. It is faithful in fulfilling its agenda, which makes available empowering meanings of anything that befalls us.

Furthermore, what if we don't just create meaning for things that happen in our lives? Consider that some scholars say we may be creating those very events and bringing those people into our lives, then we make up the story. . . they did this, they did that. In an interview with Jungian analyst and Episcopal priest John A. Sanford, a reporter for *The Sun* asked about the extent to which we create painful experiences that show up in our lives. For instance, he was asked if a boy that was bullied "called his tormentors to him?" Sanford replied, "Oh absolutely. At the unconscious level, he's sending a message about what he needs for integration." Sanford related the question to Fritz Kunkle's insight that these bullies could be archangels merely carrying out a divine plan to create that opportunity of pain the boy could channel into healing.

Whether or not the archangel construct makes sense for your spirituality, others triggering us can be a gift to remind us of the new heights we have yet to climb. It has been said that we're wounded through relationships; through them, we must heal. The apostle Paul thanks God for the thorn in his side in II Corinthians 12:7. Paul says this thorn keeps him from relying on his strength and instead depending on the Father. A part of me embraces my thorns with humor; as friends and colleagues often hear me say, the universe has given me countless opportunities to suffer and strengthen my forgiveness muscle. And strengthened it is. Thank you, universe.

COMING HOME TO THE BIRDSEYE VIEW

Having shed false views, and continuing to practice the integration offered, we strengthen our capacity to hold new realities, entering new levels of consciousness. We discover a peace that abounds within our being that's so freeing, we want more of it. Perhaps we're finally liberated from the shackles that have held us hostage to a life filled with unnecessary suffering, on this side of Eden. *A Course in Miracles* refers to this process as "waking up from the dream."

When we look upon our fellow human beings, instead of seeing just the physical, we see the formless and nameless part of their being. We play with the world of form, but we realize that our identities and those of others aren't bound by form. The changeless part of us, the part as we may refer to as spirit, sees that part in the other, and then the purpose for having taken the journey makes sense. We feel connected in this new realm.

Like so many wonders that can only be experienced instead of explained to truly feel their magnitude (electricity, wind, rain, a certain color, the sunrise), we sense this new level of consciousness when we arrive and embody it. Have you seen one sunset that was so captivating it took your breath away and moved you to experience a joy you never knew existed? That new experience is encoded and locked into your delicate nervous system. Likewise, once we see our oneness, we can't unsee the majesty of being in perfect peace in the mind and body.

Sounds amazing, right? But how will we know we're moving toward higher levels of consciousness? Here's a litmus test: Think about a person that the very idea of them used to repulse you (the homeless person on the corner), anger you (your mother-in-law), or fill you with contempt (your boss). Having gone through the journey in this book, think of one of those people and notice if you're triggered. If not, you may well be growing in a higher level of consciousness.

If you are triggered, that can be a blessing. You've discovered another place to heal. Notice where the hurt originates. Zoom in and observe the tender place that was dinged with its negative cognition and somatic sensations. Perhaps it's, "I am powerless." Don't judge it. Just notice it. Next, zoom out and take a birdseye view to access a part of yourself that sees beyond your hurt, into the core of their being. Any thought or feeling that attempts to seduce you back into the old stuck patterns of the mind are lower levels of consciousness feeding you false beliefs of fear, scarcity, and separateness. Notice them, and with love and tenderness, from this new place of being, move through the steps with wisdom and precision to escort them through the door of your mind. Every time you do this, you increase your wholeness.

The more we practice residing in this level of consciousness, the more effortless it becomes. Freedom from triggers isn't the point; we're moving toward freedom from staying stuck in suffering. We will know we are experiencing the birdseye view when:

- We get dinged by a zinger, but we don't stay stuck there

- We weep with others

- We experience less suffering and
  more compassion

I leave you with a description of the place of being where we recognize ourselves in every other living being and them in us. The beloved monk Thich Nat Hahn writes:

> I am a frog swimming happily in the clear water of a pond. I am also the grass snake who approaching in silence feeds himself on the frog. I am the child in Uganda, all skin and bones my legs as thin as bamboo sticks. I am also the merchant of arms selling deadly weapons to Uganda. I am the twelve-year girl refugee in a small boat who throws herself into the ocean after being raped by a sea pirate. I am also the see pirate; my heart not yet capable of seeing and loving. My joy is like spring. It makes flowers bloom in all walks of life. My pain is like a river of tears; so full it fills up all the four oceans. Please call me by my correct name so I can hear at the same time all my cries and my laughs. So that I can see that my joy and pain are but one. Please call me by my correct names so that I may become awake. So, the door of my heart be left open. The door of compassion.

POINTS OF CONTEMPLATION

Ready to practice residing in the place of "to know all is to forgive all?" Reflect on the following questions to imagine the gift of the birdseye view.

- Connect with your place within that holds the "knowing." Close your eyes and notice what's different when you reach this place within your being. Journal about any shifts in thought, feeling, or perception.

- Try to lay still and meditate on saying goodbye to everything and everyone you know. Notice any difference in the things/identities you have clung to so tightly. How can you bring this feeling of freedom from overidentification of ego states forward into your life?

- Look around you the next time you're with a group. Try to look beyond the form to the formless. Then write about your experience. Could you see the spirit within the other? How? What did you notice in yourself?

Zenest of the Zen

Numerous times throughout writing this manuscript, I found myself saying to my husband humorously, "I'm going to be the first one to read my book," as in, *I continue to need these reminders as much as the next person!* We would both chuckle at how this journey isn't one-and-done where you reached your destination, and you're an enlightened being, so here's your certificate of completion—thank you for attending the workshop. Did you turn to this page and hope there was a box to check? A symbol denoting that you mastered the dynamics of your inner world and interpersonal and intrapersonal relationships, never to take anything personally ever again? Well, we haven't arrived, and we never will. This process is an ongoing journey requiring patience, emotional presence, and compassion for the self.

Perhaps before reading this book, you felt clueless as to why the actions and words of others clung to you like saran wrap, gripping the circuitous self-critical mind-chatter towards the self (or the other). Now you know that the roots of taking things personally are tied to belief systems deeply engrained in neuropathways laid down long ago. Those scripts were written by someone else and imposed upon you outside your control. Thanks to neuroplasticity, we can rewrite these scripts. This book fortifies us with a sense of agency over our reactions formerly caught in the undertow of insecurity, confusion, and frustration. Now, we need not be thrown off balance or pulled into despair by the zingers that come our way or our projections onto others and meaning-making through a narrow lens.

In this book, we encompassed "forgiveness" and its sticky connotations. Some of those ideas were revealed as mistaken beliefs that we must sacrifice parts of the self that most needed tending, leading to spiritual bypasses in a rush to forgive. And while we validated that our coloring of the word is skewed by distorted scripts connected to our primal attachment framework, we also embraced a radical shift to view ourselves and the other more clearly. Our power lies in widening the gap between trigger and default reaction where we can exercise greater free will. No longer pointing a finger at others and giving our power away, we can make a U-turn and look within. There, we find a healthier way to dance with forgiveness: Instead of demanding justice before peace is possible, we redefine the paradigm to create justice for the inner child by giving them a voice and holding healthy boundaries.

You're invited into a more profound human experience. *It's Never Personal* has illuminated the higher road to the highest place–the apex of spiritual and psychological evolution, the birdseye view. Here, we're free from mental constructs and distorted views of self and others; true peace resides. Our newfound wholeness sets us up to move against the usual currents of human behavior into higher heights, manifesting in our ability to extend compassion to those who, in the world's view, are undeserving of mercy or grace. Yes, having removed obstructions within the self, we're shored up to be a light unto the path of the other. Love flows more easily through us now, and we flourish more in creativity, joy, and vitality.

More than likely, no one reaches this point in the book and confidently claims they're the next spiritual guru. The Zenest of the Zen. We're not bulletproof from the slings arrows of life. Yet, we can't unlearn the messages, stories, and teachings in these pages. After reading this book, we can't pretend to have no responsibility to love ourselves and our fellow humans well. Not heeding this call might be considered foolish at best. We are called. We aren't fools. The wisest readers will seek professional therapy to continue learning and practicing the NPP steps.

Carry your expanded understanding of forgiveness with you. May you continue to grow in wisdom, peace, and free will. Remember, you can return at any time to your place of knowing that "I don't know." Here, we inhabit the truth that *there is nothing to forgive.*

Acknowledgments

I am moved beyond words by the love, encouragement, and support I received from family, friends, and colleagues throughout the very rewarding journey of writing this book. First, a word of acknowledgment to the beta readers who provided fruitful feedback as I continued to put the finishing touches on the teachings of the Never Personal Process. I wanted to ensure the message was clear and easily digestible, and you helped me do so. Thank you! I remain deeply touched by your unselfish commitment—bringing heart, mind, and spirit—to help me see this message through the lens of the reader. Your words of encouragement along the way gave me inspiration to continue dedicating energy and focus to this book. Receiving feedback such as, "I think everyone in the world should read this book. If they did, the world would be a better place", further solidified my conviction in wanting to get this book into the readers' hands. So, Becca Taft, Jill Hamilton, Katie DeAscanis, Renée Flamand, Vicky Crenshaw, Lindsey Coates Horvatich, Mike Custer, Christy Cheney, Lesley MacIntosh, Teona Alexander, Todd Budgen, Mark Beck, Leslie Larson, and Diane Kimball, thank you.

A special thanks to Roger Shepherd, who has walked alongside me through life's darkest valleys, some of which I write about in this book. He has been, not just one of my supervisors in my master's program, but a friend, counselor, mentor, and spiritual guru. During supervision, while staffing a client's case we supervisees commonly asked in a lighthearted way, "What would Roger say? Roger, thank you for helping me find my equilibrium when life pulled the rug out from underneath me: You are gifted in speaking wisdom and dignity into the lives of others, and you have had a profound presence in my life.

I am deeply grateful for my editor, Cindy Childress. From the beginning, you patiently walked alongside a first-time author with brilliant insight into my vision for the message I wanted to get out to the world. Your grace and talent far exceeded my expectations throughout the process, as you wore more than just an "editor's" hat; you served as a gifted mentor and coach as well. May other authors have the opportunity to be wrapped in the incredible experience of being in your energy field. You are the real deal!

To my parents, who, while no longer with us in the world of form, remain ever-present in my heart and mind, continuing to shape me. Thanks to you, I am a human who cares deeply for my fellow humans, embodies a level of humor, light, and joy that keeps life interesting, and always stays on the path of seeking truth and wisdom. Thank you, Mom, for the reminders that I can do anything in life I put my mind to. For that gift, I often don't see limits of dreams and possibilities the way others often do. For the wisdom that others say I behold, I never miss an opportunity to credit my mother, who, to this day, is still being spoken of as one of the wisest woman among all who knew her.

A most special thanks to my husband. After reading the intro to the manuscript early in the project, you became my biggest cheerleader. Thank you, Michael. Thank you for believing in my qualities, my heart, and my important, special, and unique message to share with the world.

I would be remiss if I did not thank the infinite wisdom of the universe (and my shadow self) for bringing people and situations into my path that have invited me deeper into the process of integration, compassion, empathy, and enlightenment. Through feeling rejection, betrayal, and abandonment by others, the darkest nights of my soul have truly brought and continue to bring about profound growth. That pain helps me continue to find ways to heal the wounds of the heart, providing the scaffolding for this book and the Never Personal Process.

About the Author

Victoria Kennedy believes we come into the world with an innateness to thrive, feel fully alive, and be creative. Somewhere along the way, whether in childhood or adulthood, we may experience some level of pain or disappointment that makes us forget our human dignity and be someone we're not. For her, this culminated in pleasing her father with a major in business, not philosophy or psychology; twenty years later, an epic heartbreak and betrayal catapulted her into a master's program in counseling. Finally, as she followed her bliss in becoming a relationship expert, she was on a path that aligned with her spirit.

As a licensed psychotherapist, Victoria has the pleasure of helping couples and individuals illuminate mysteries of their complex inner worlds—the world of emotions, thoughts, and behaviors—and find the way back to their authentic selves. She considers walking with her clients along their darkest times to be sacred ground. Known by peers and clients for delivering complex concepts in an easily digestible and relatable manner, her clients have dubbed her "Vicki Buddha," "Mind Ninja," and "Sherpa" to name a few.

She's Certified in Emotionally Focused Therapy, known as the gold standard in couples and family therapy. Her work as a relationship expert includes facilitating transformational Hold Me Tight Workshops for Couples, both in the United States and internationally. Her completed advanced trainings include: Sex and EFT, Ego State Work, Pre-Verbal Work, and working with betrayals. She is also a Certified Grief Counselor.

When not facilitating a workshop or seeing clients, Victoria enjoys playing piano (sometimes attempting to write her own music), playing tennis, and traveling. She frequently goes hiking and boating with her husband and rescue dogs (Beckham and Chachi), splitting their time between Florida and Western North Carolina. Fluent in Spanish, she adores spending time with family both in the U.S. and Spain. After years of practice and breaking the budget on lessons in piano and tennis, she's learned to take deep breaths and stay very humble; reminding herself that staying emotionally present in the process is more important than being overly invested in the outcome. As her mother used to say, "We all need to learn to walk through life with our heads a little lower."